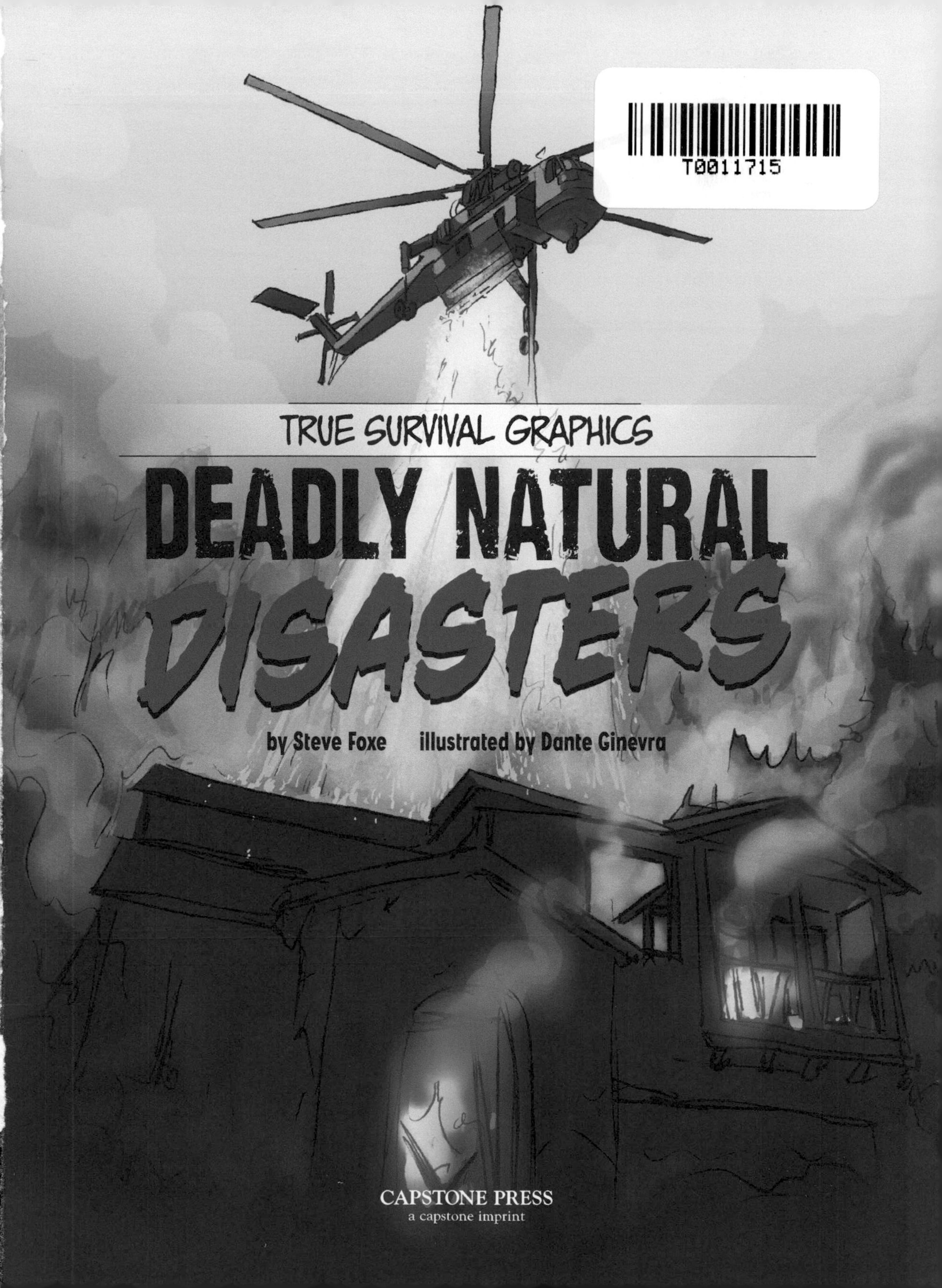

TRUE SURVIVAL GRAPHICS

DEADLY NATURAL DISASTERS

by Steve Foxe illustrated by Dante Ginevra

CAPSTONE PRESS
a capstone imprint

Published by Capstone Press, an imprint of Capstone
1710 Roe Crest Drive, North Mankato, Minnesota 56003
capstonepub.com

Library of Congress Cataloging-in-Publication Data
Names: Foxe, Steve, author. | Ginevra, Dante, 1976– illustrator.
Title: Deadly natural disasters / by Steve Foxe ; illustrated by Dante Ginevra.
Description: North Mankato, Minnesota : Capstone Press, [2024] | Series: True survival graphics | Includes bibliographical references. | Audience: Ages 9–11 | Audience: Grades 4–6 | Summary: "A massive tsunami slams into a tourist's train. A violent volcanic eruption overwhelms a hiker with hot ash and gases. A raging wildfire forces a family to flee without their beloved animals. These deadly natural disasters ended in tragedy for some-but not everyone. How did the people in these true tales come face to face with the forces of nature and live to tell about it?"—Provided by publisher.
Identifiers: LCCN 2023014739 (print) | LCCN 2023014740 (ebook) | ISBN 9781669058687 (hardcover) | ISBN 9781669058939 (paperback) | ISBN 9781669058946 (pdf) | ISBN 9781669058960 (kindle edition) | ISBN 9781669058953 (epub)
Subjects: LCSH: Natural disasters—Juvenile literature. | Natural disasters—Comic books, strips, etc. | LCGFT: Nonfiction comics. | Graphic novels.
Classification: LCC GB5019 .F69 2024 (print) | LCC GB5019 (ebook) | DDC 363.34—dc23/eng/20230512
LC record available at https://lccn.loc.gov/2023014739
LC ebook record available at https://lccn.loc.gov/2023014740

Editorial Credits
Editor: Christopher Harbo; Designer: Tracy Davies;
Production Specialist: Katy LaVigne

All internet sites appearing in back matter were available and accurate when this book was sent to press.

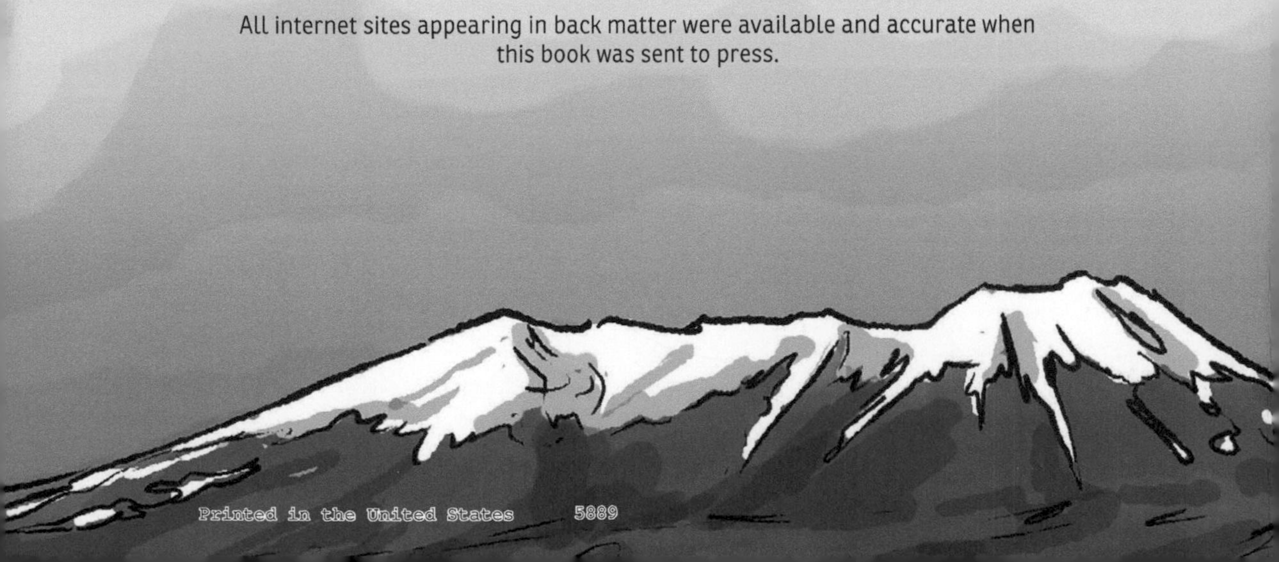

Printed in the United States 5889

TABLE OF CONTENTS

INTRODUCTION

DISASTER AWAITS!

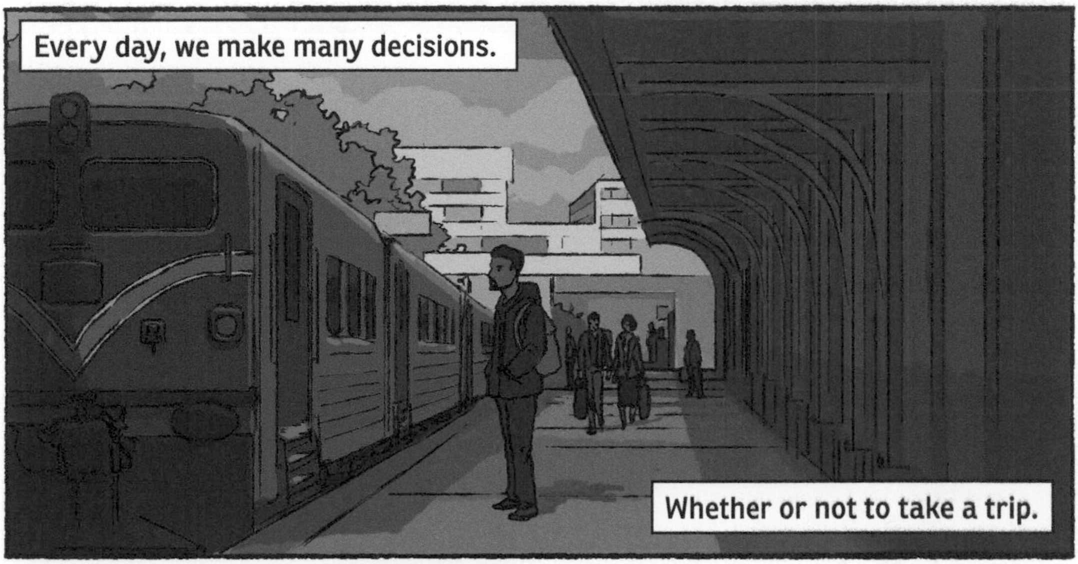
Every day, we make many decisions.
Whether or not to take a trip.

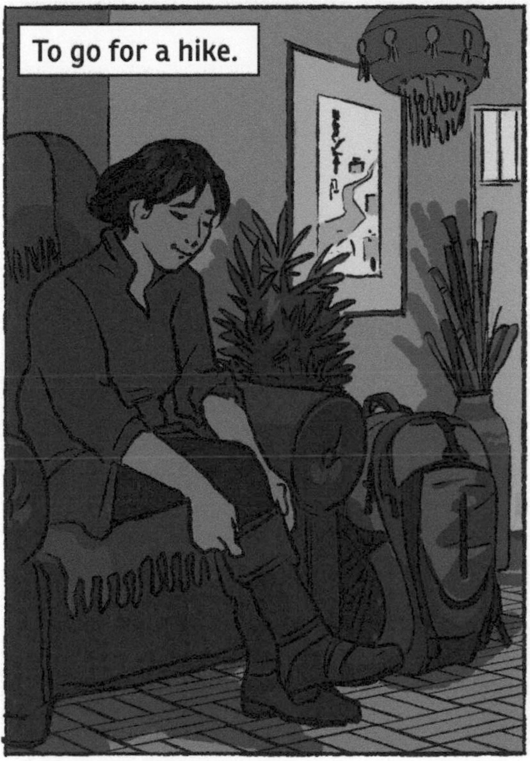
To go for a hike.

Or to spend time at home with family and pets.

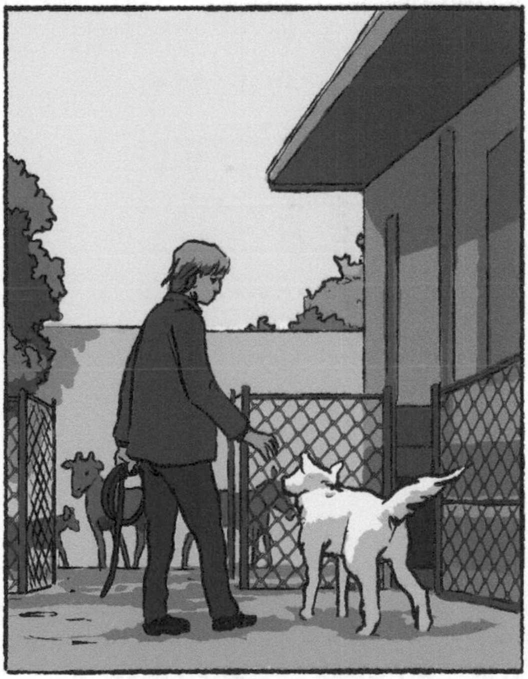

And every day, disaster can strike without warning.

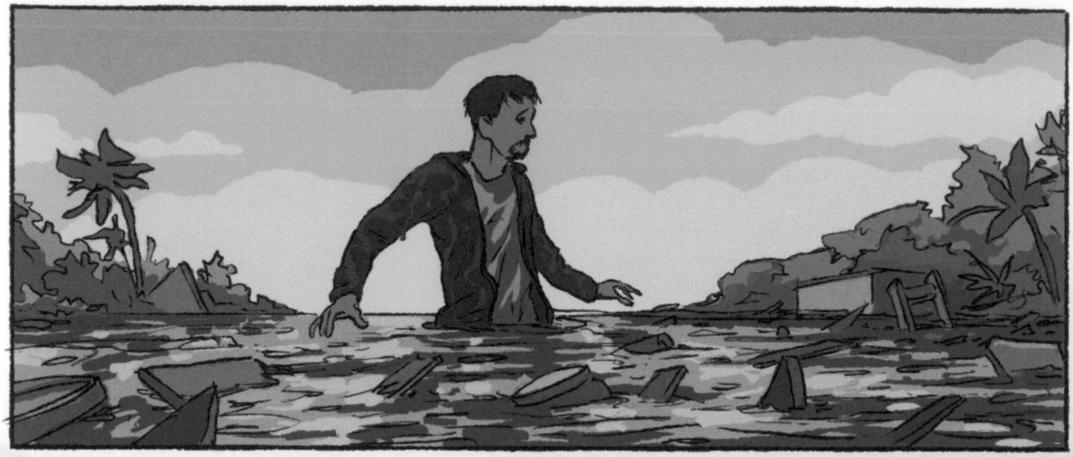

Survival can be a matter of planning, gut feelings, and luck.

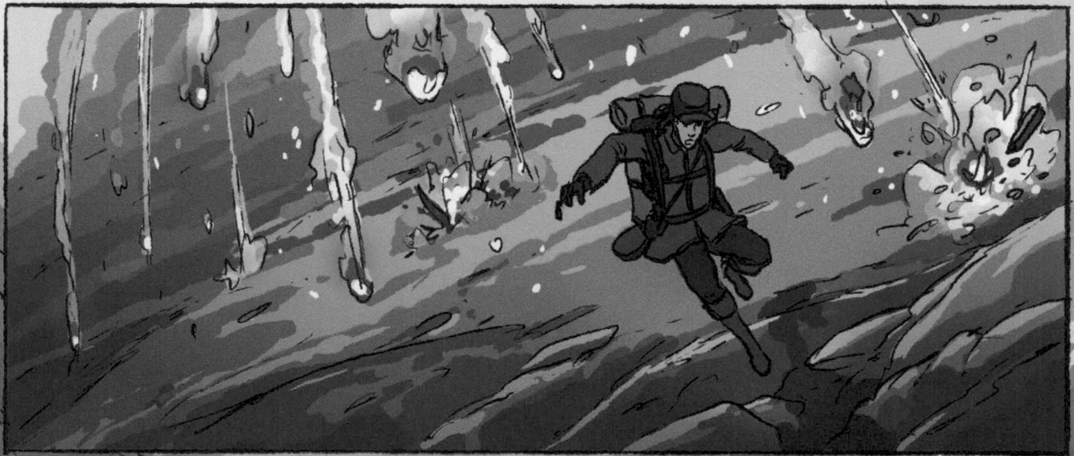

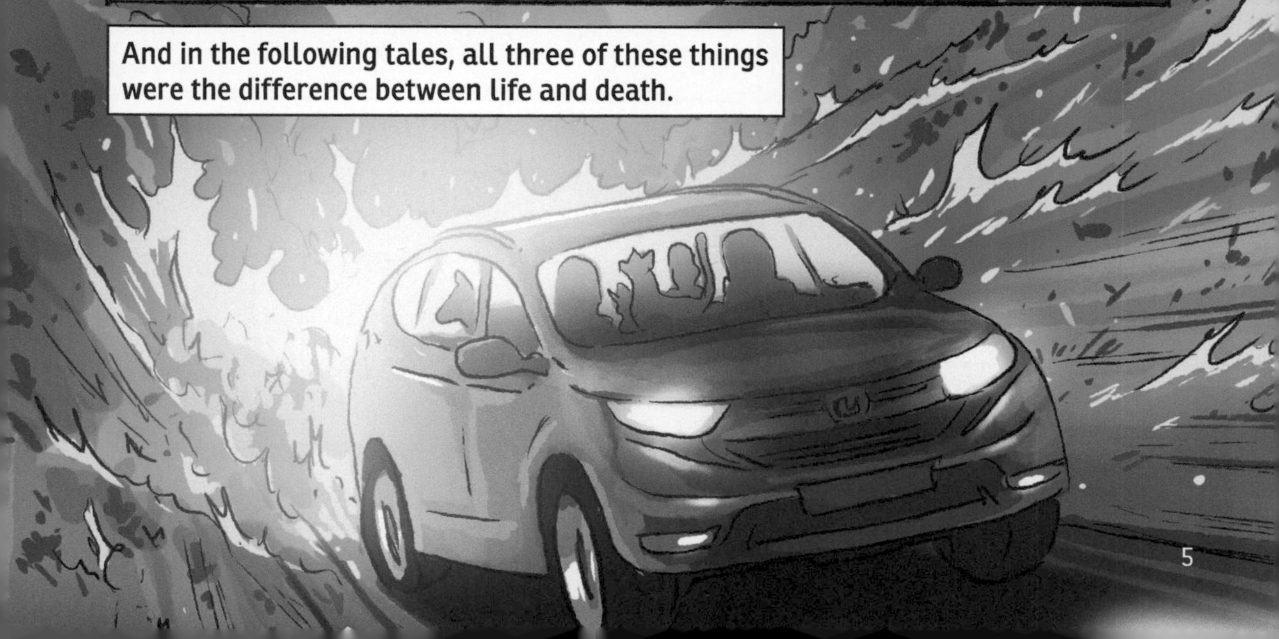
And in the following tales, all three of these things were the difference between life and death.

CHAPTER 1

TSUNAMI TERROR!

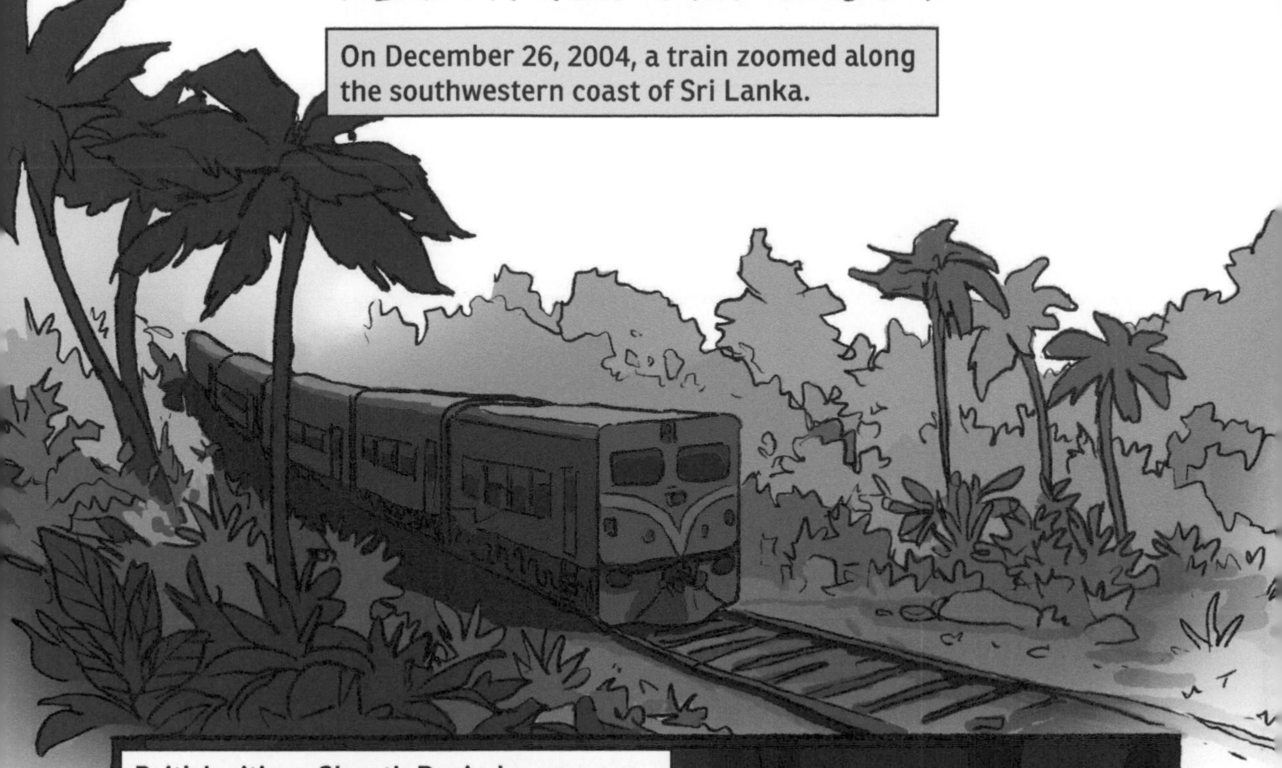
On December 26, 2004, a train zoomed along the southwestern coast of Sri Lanka.

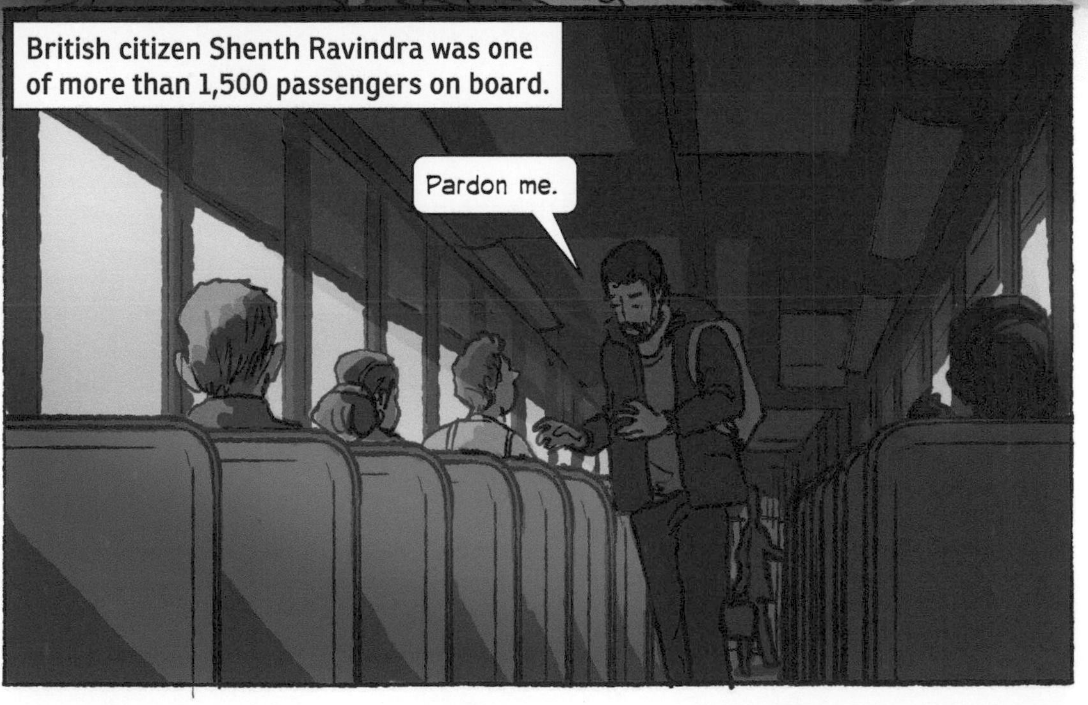
British citizen Shenth Ravindra was one of more than 1,500 passengers on board.
Pardon me.

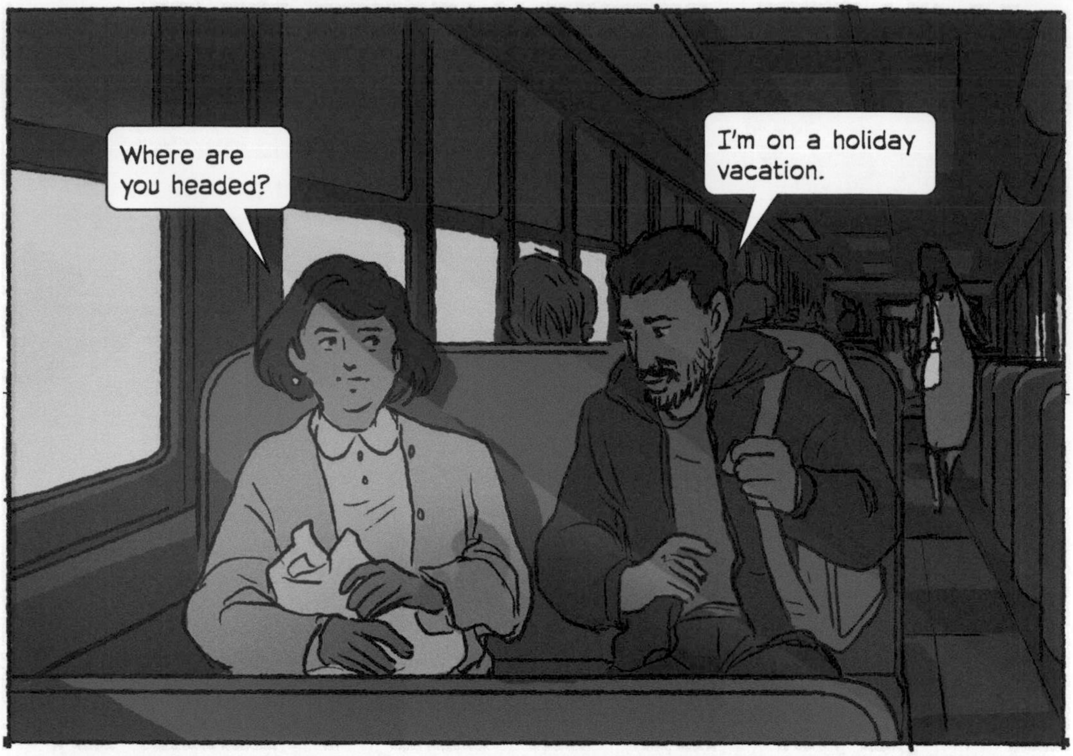
Where are you headed?
I'm on a holiday vacation.

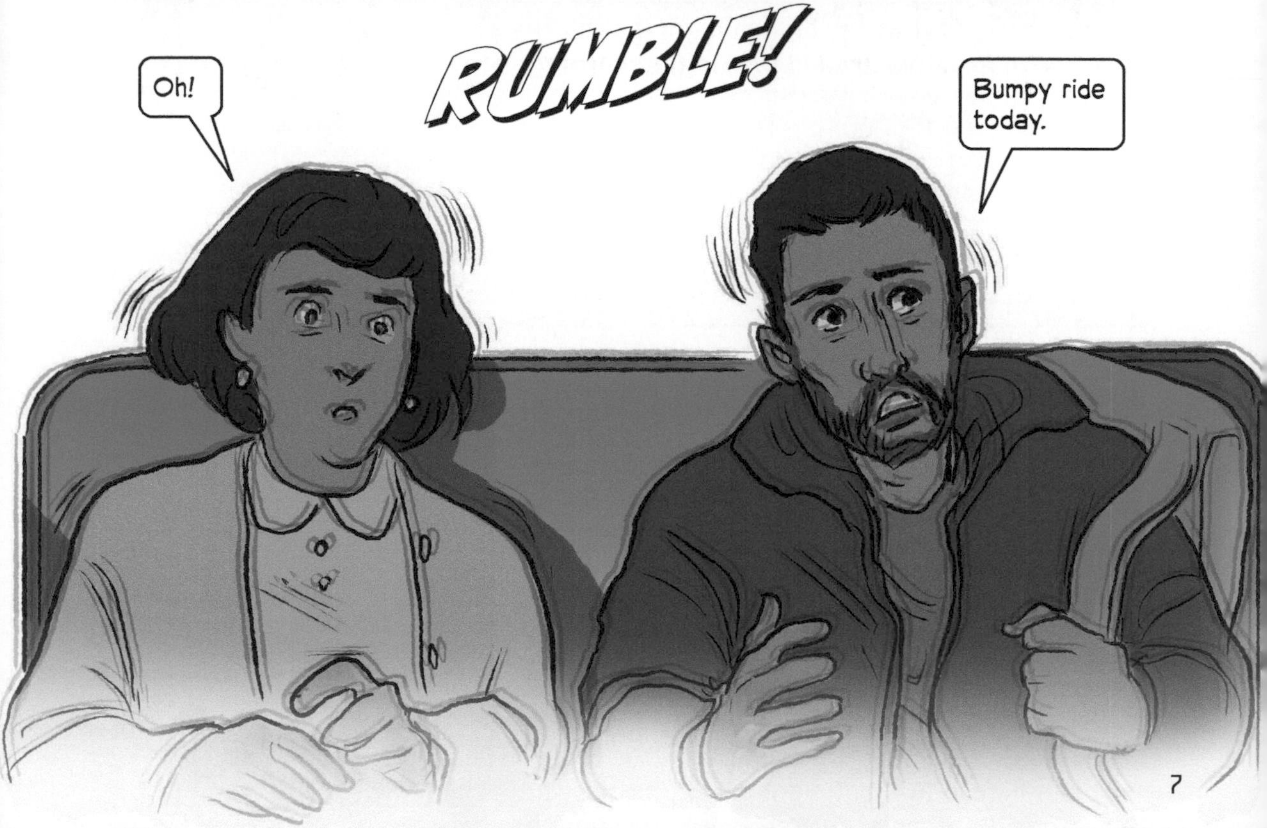
Oh!
RUMBLE!
Bumpy ride today.

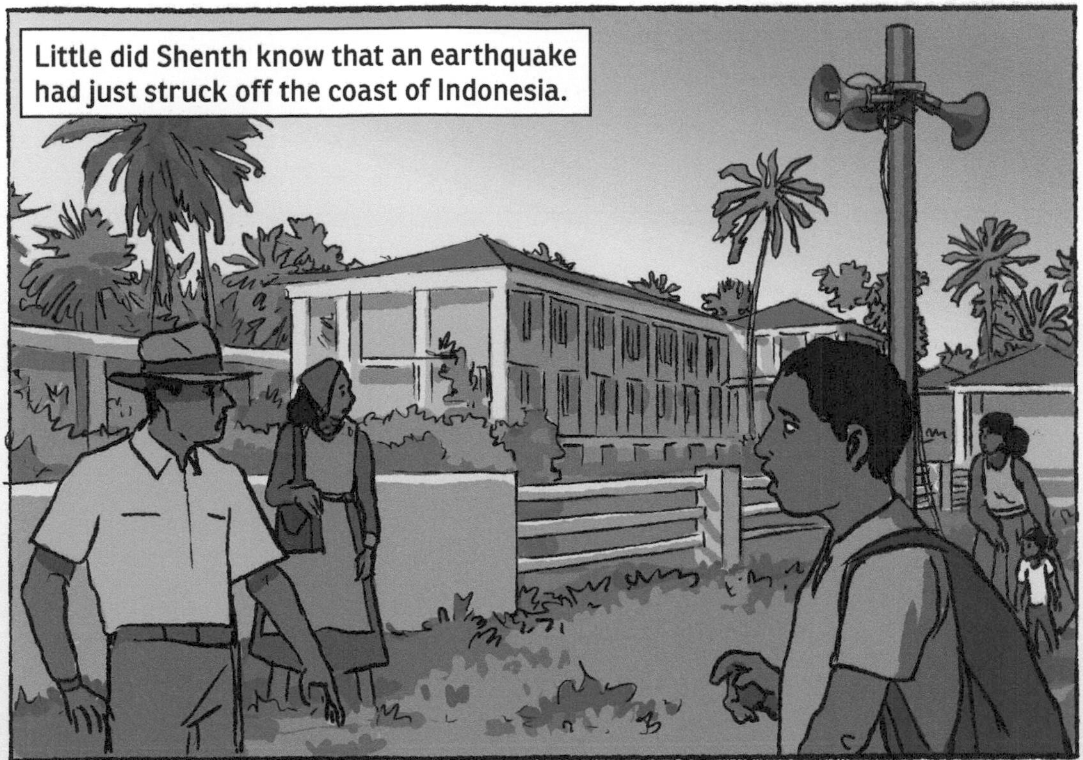
Little did Shenth know that an earthquake had just struck off the coast of Indonesia.

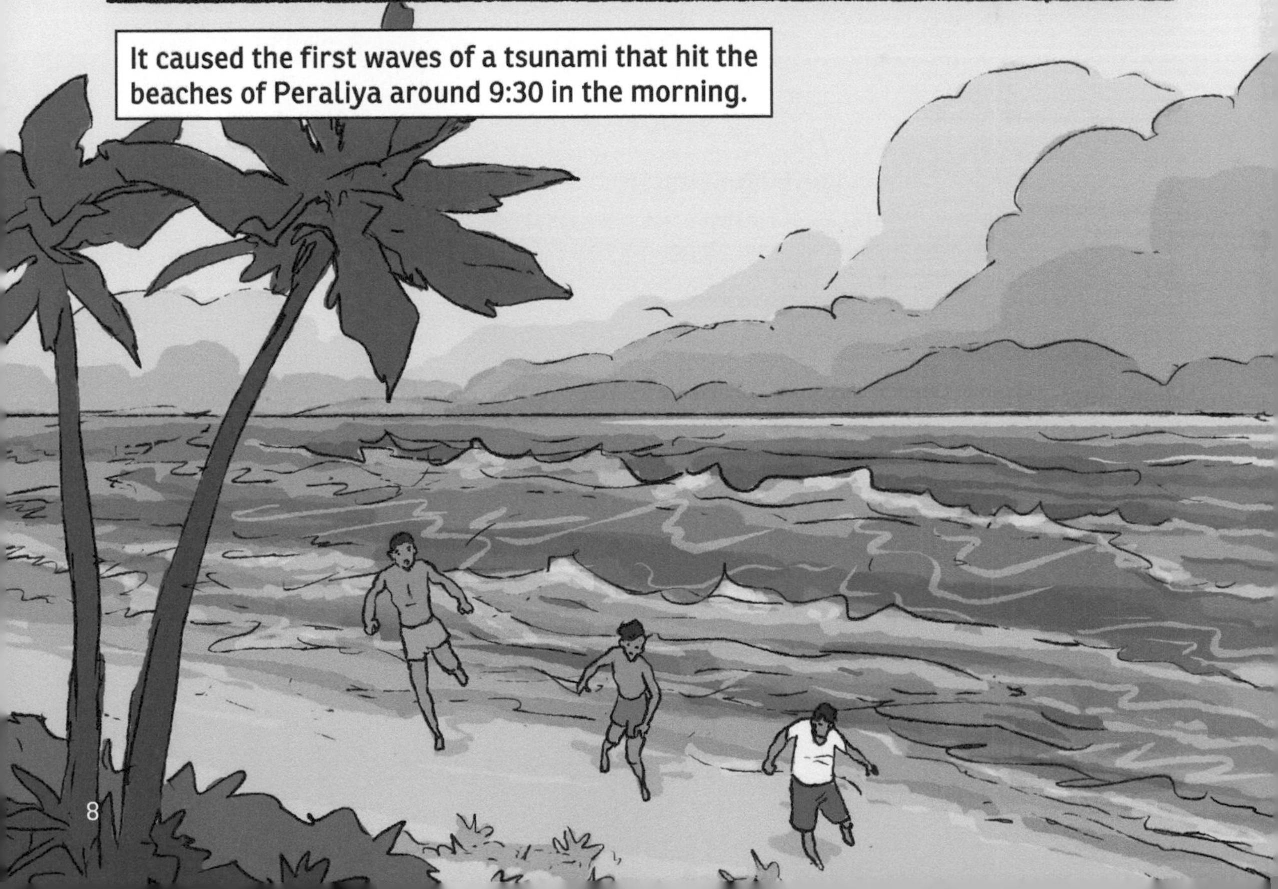
It caused the first waves of a tsunami that hit the beaches of Peraliya around 9:30 in the morning.

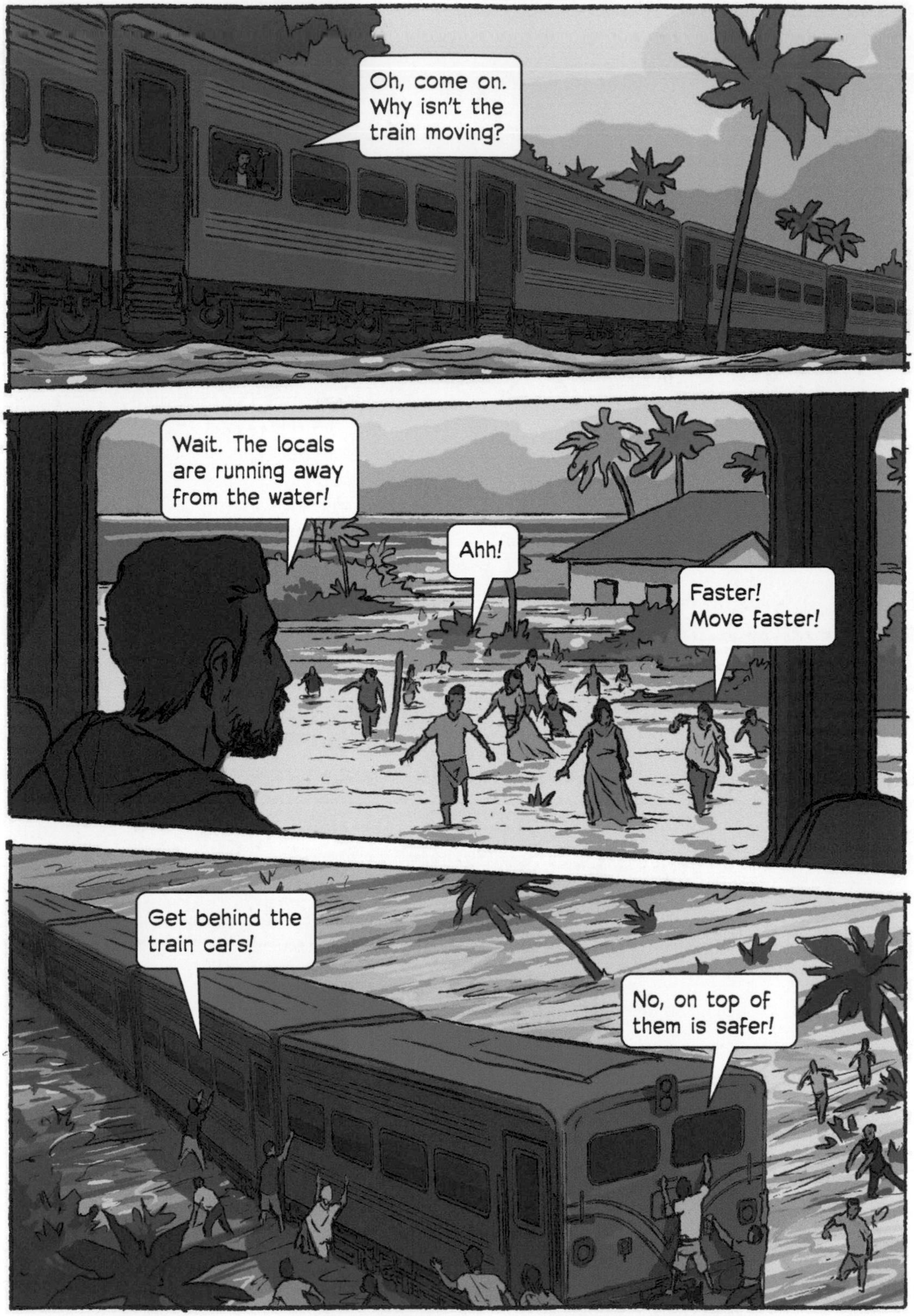
Oh, come on. Why isn't the train moving?
Wait. The locals are running away from the water!
Ahh!
Faster! Move faster!
Get behind the train cars!
No, on top of them is safer!

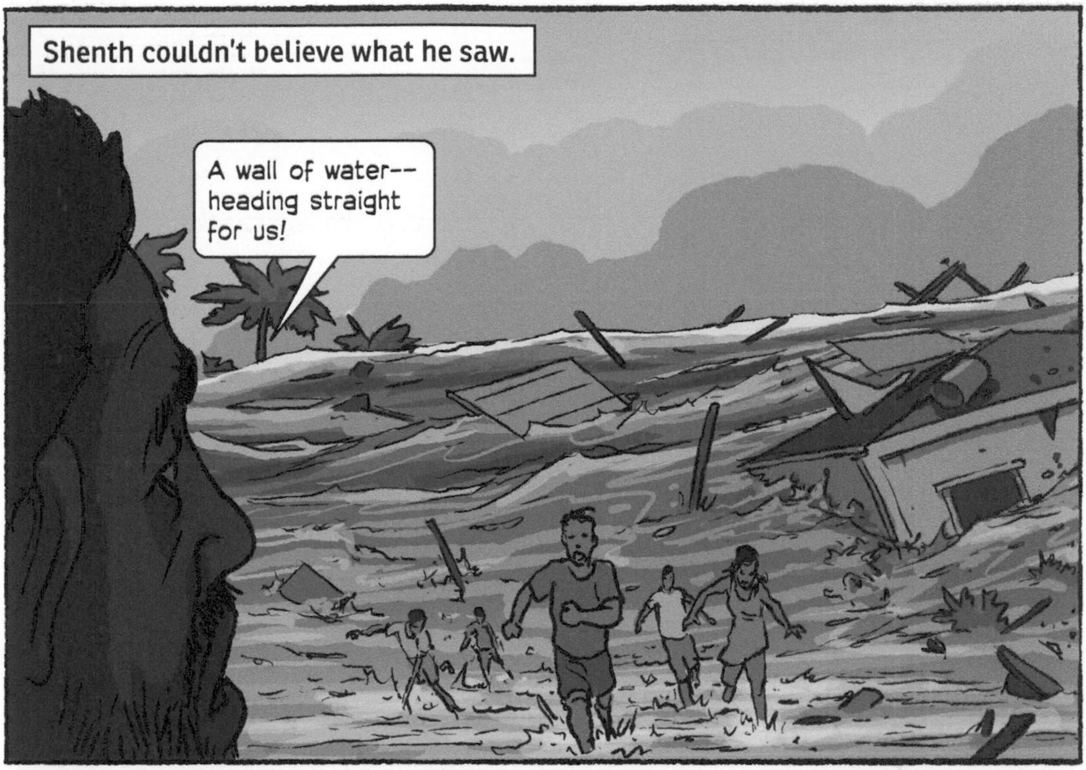
Shenth couldn't believe what he saw.
A wall of water-- heading straight for us!

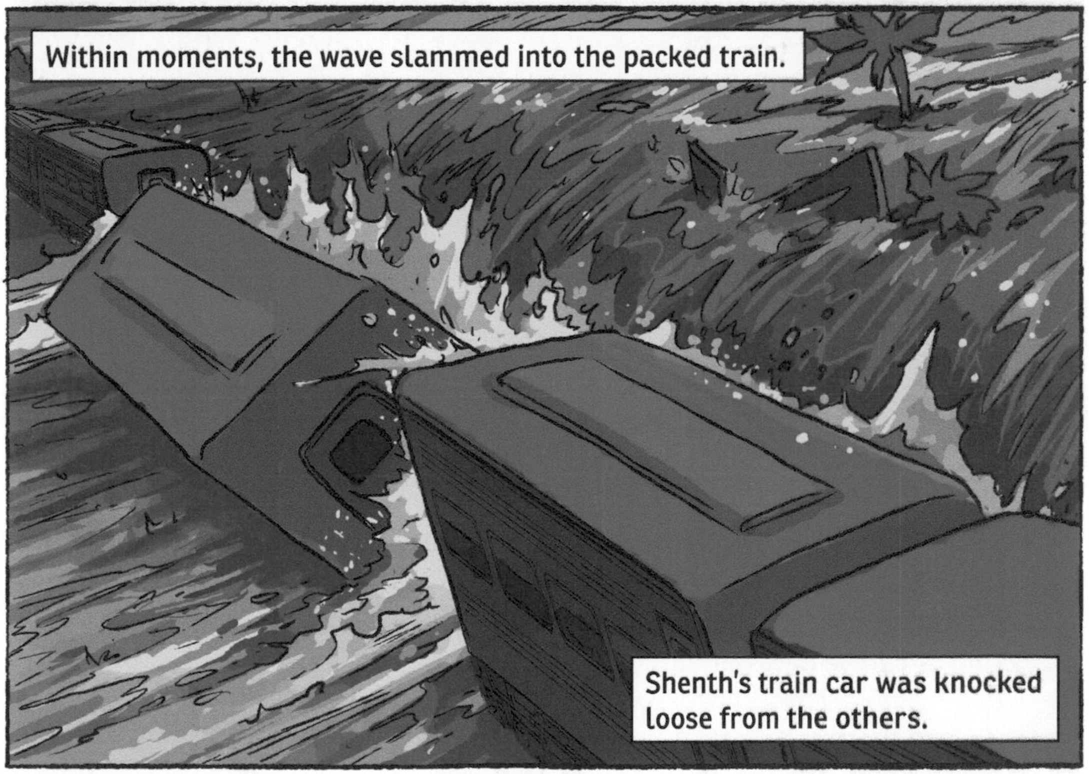
Within moments, the wave slammed into the packed train.
Shenth's train car was knocked loose from the others.

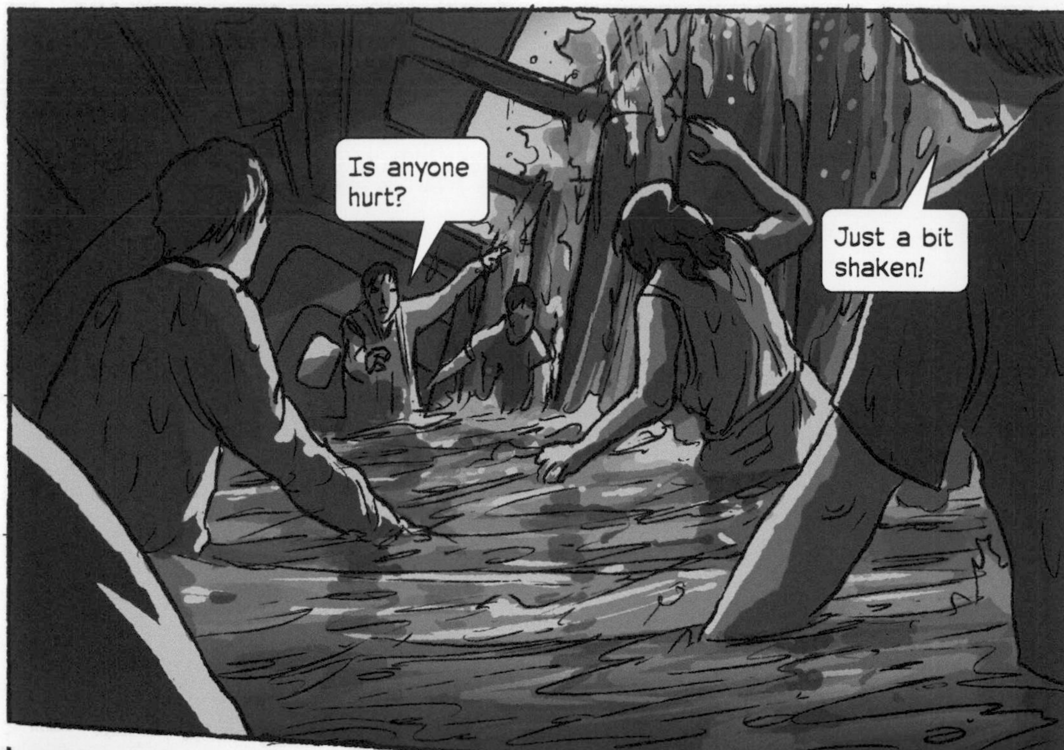
Is anyone hurt?
Just a bit shaken!

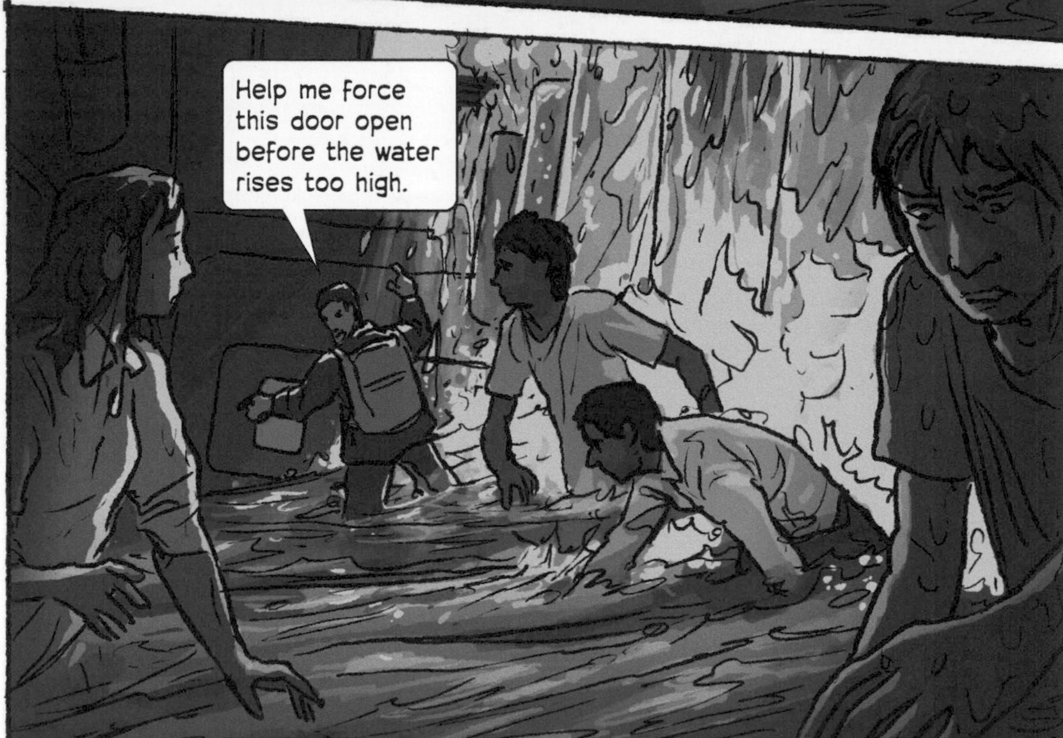
Help me force this door open before the water rises too high.

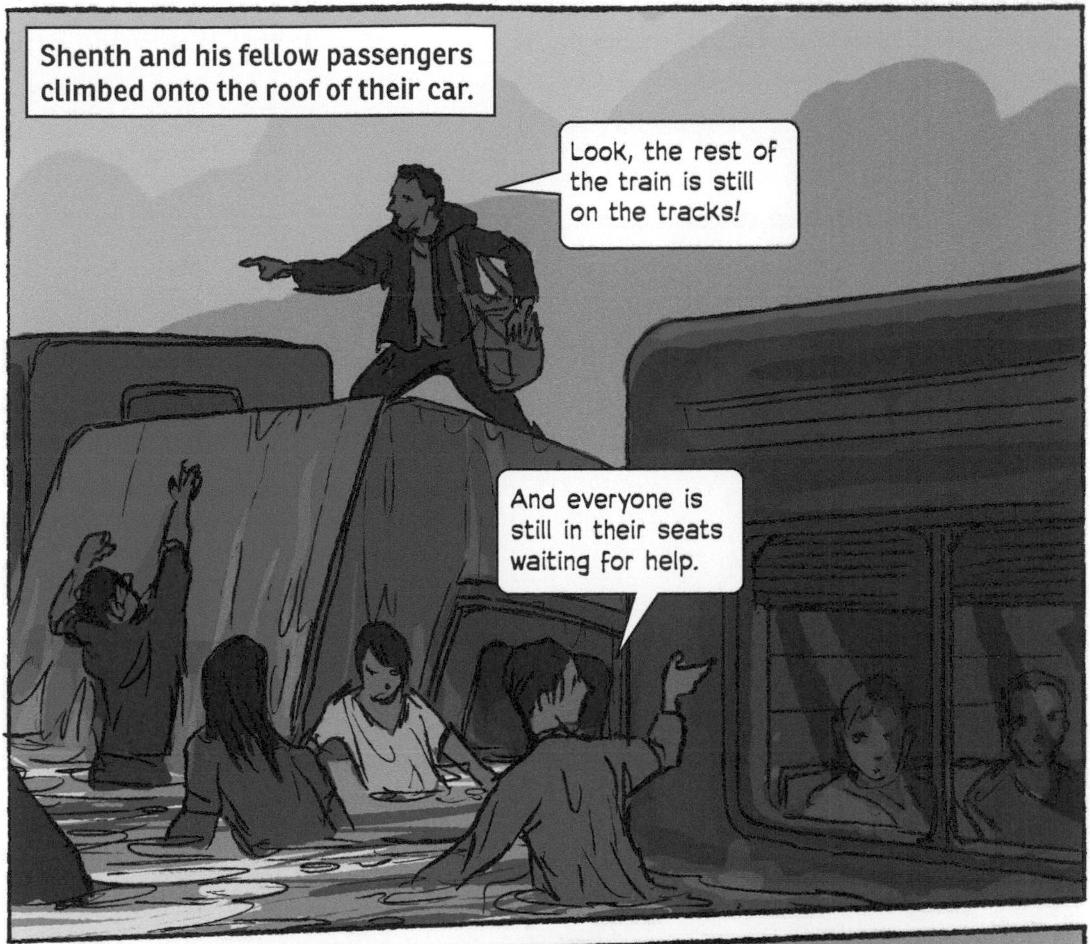
Shenth and his fellow passengers climbed onto the roof of their car.
Look, the rest of the train is still on the tracks!
And everyone is still in their seats waiting for help.

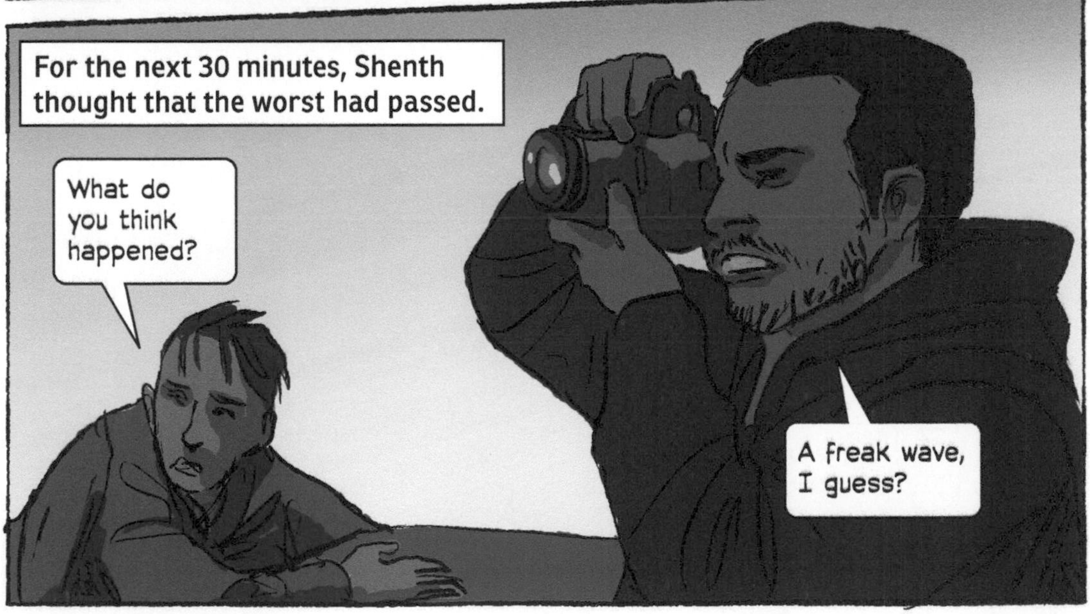
For the next 30 minutes, Shenth thought that the worst had passed.
What do you think happened?
A freak wave, I guess?

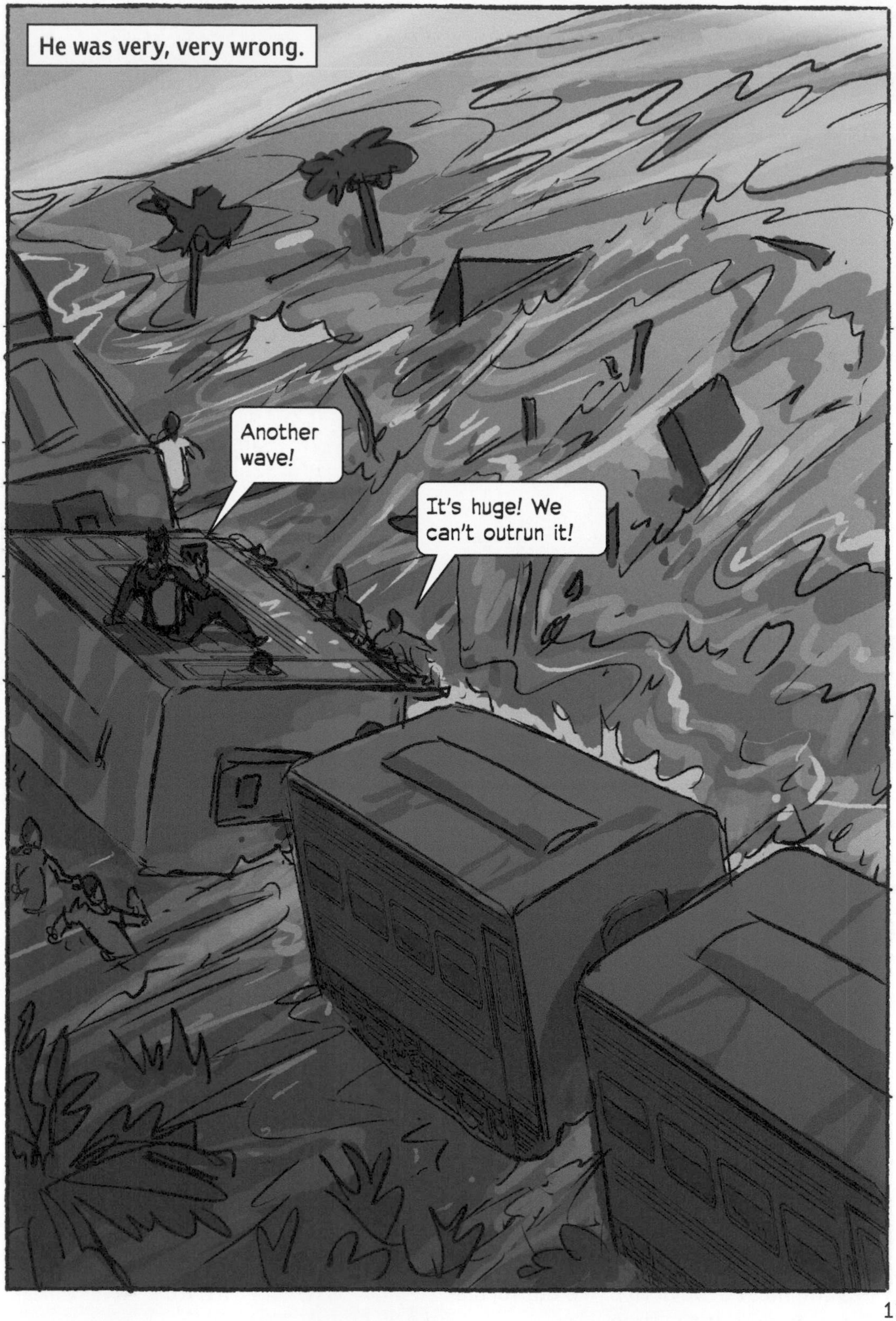
He was very, very wrong.
Another wave!
It's huge! We can't outrun it!

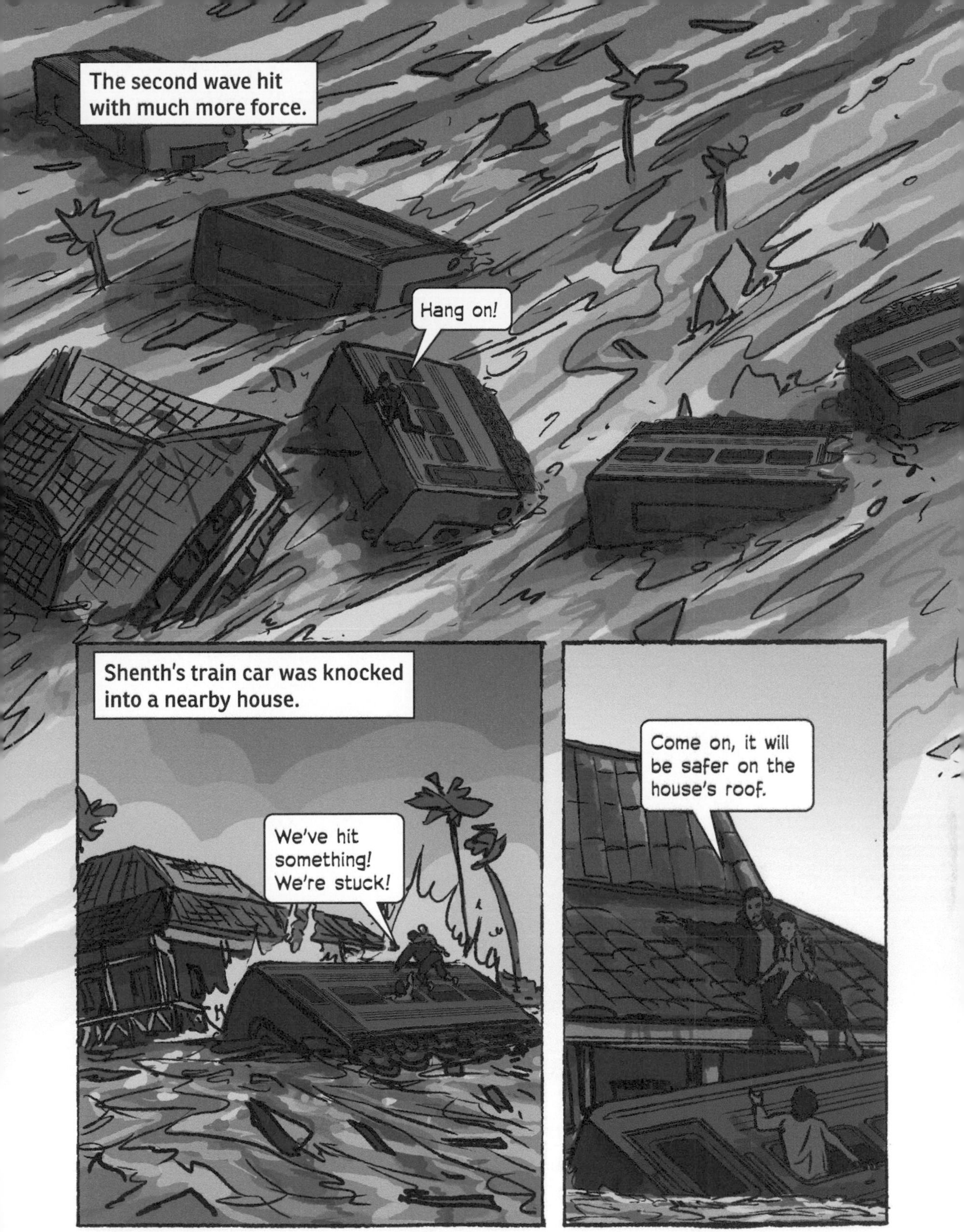
The second wave hit
with much more force.
Hang on!
Shenth's train car was knocked
into a nearby house.
We've hit
something!
We're stuck!
Come on, it will
be safer on the
house's roof.

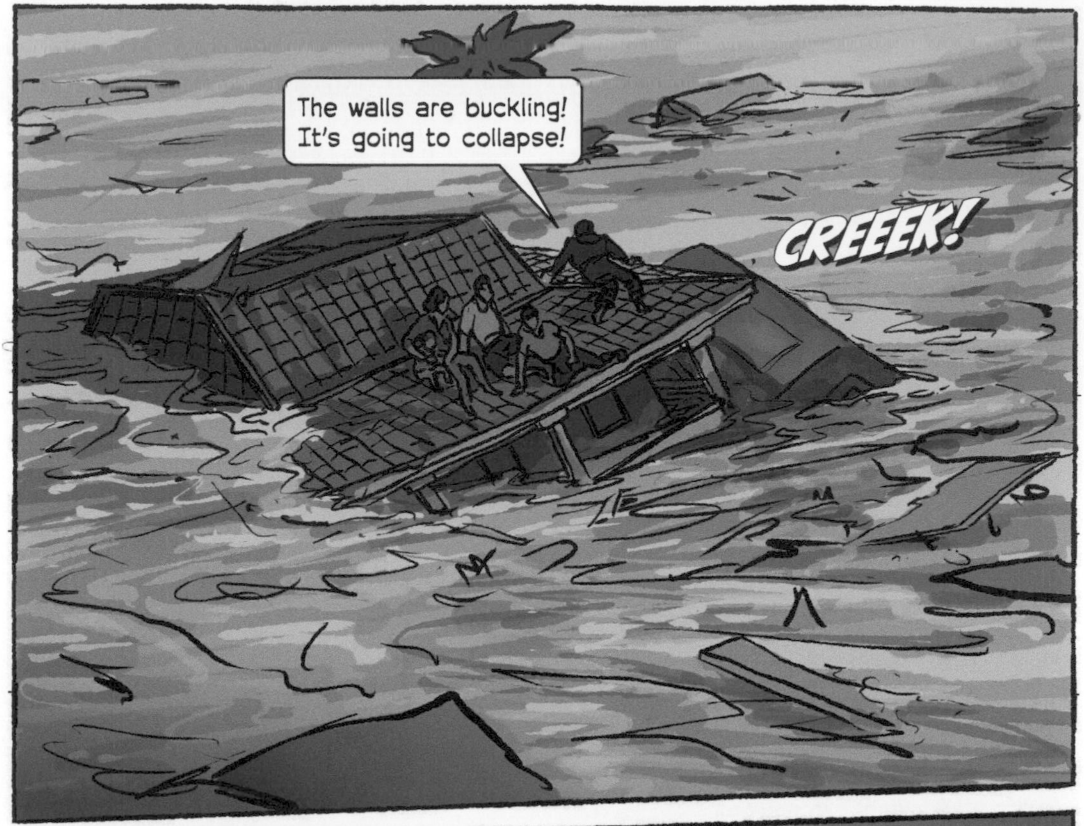
The walls are buckling! It's going to collapse!
CREEEK!

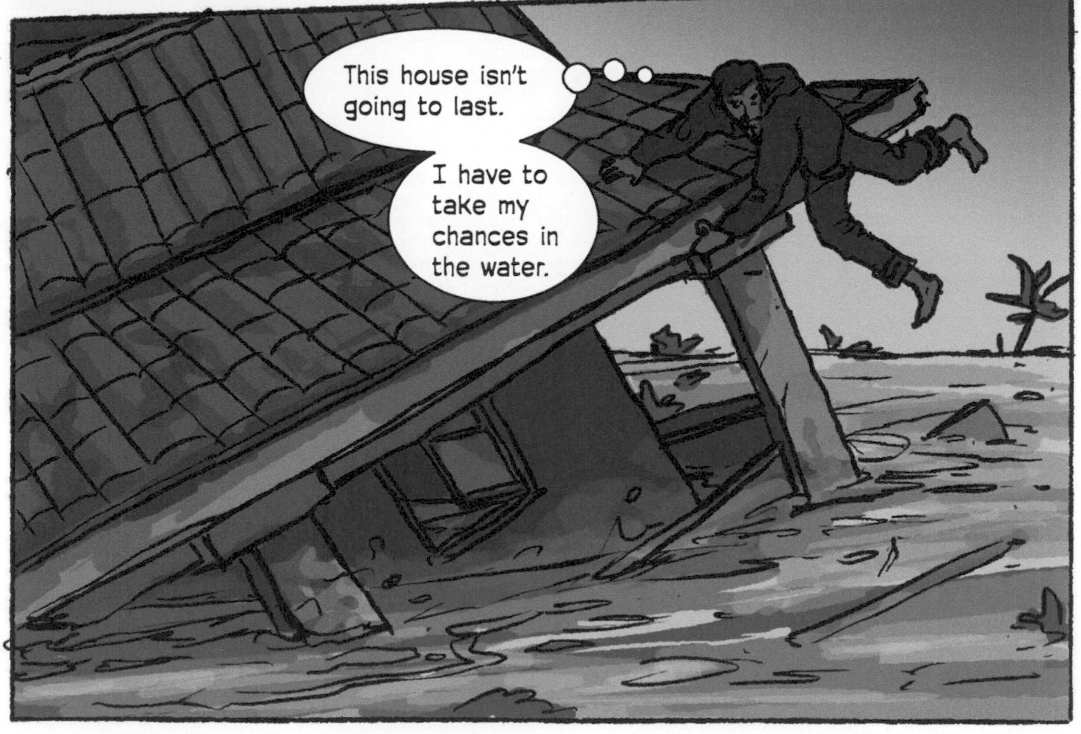
This house isn't going to last.
I have to take my chances in the water.

Shenth waded through the dirty, debris-filled water.

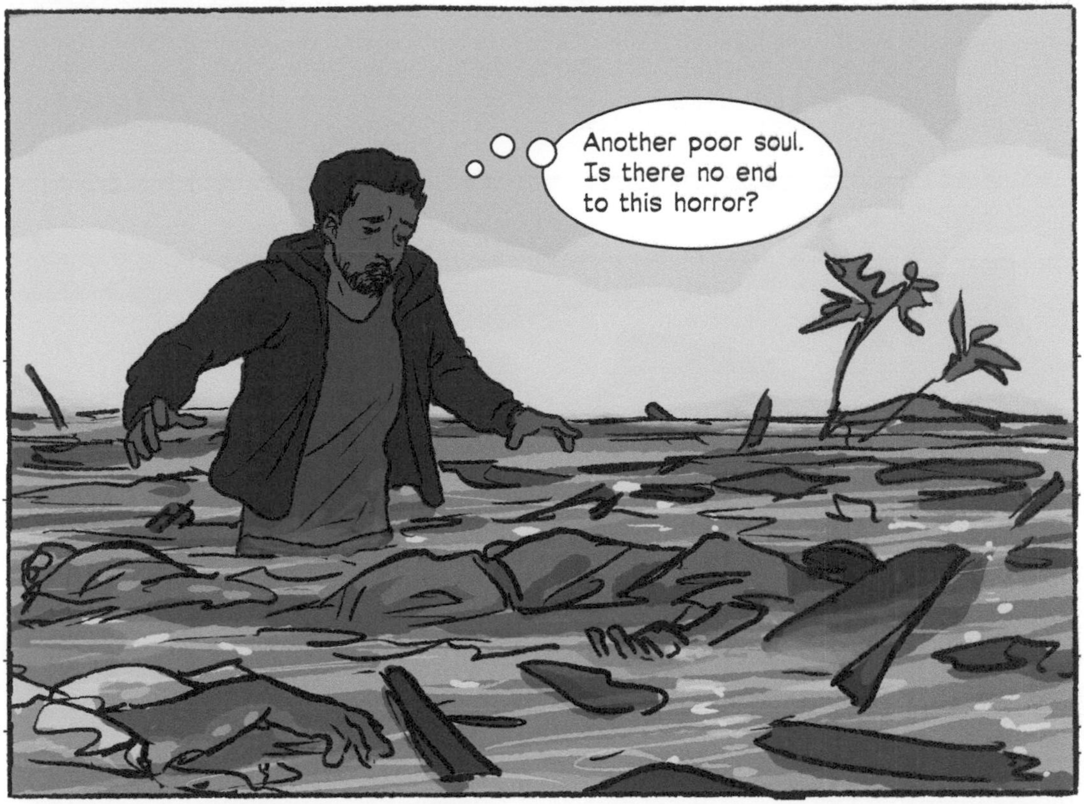
Another poor soul. Is there no end to this horror?

At one point, he sliced his foot open.

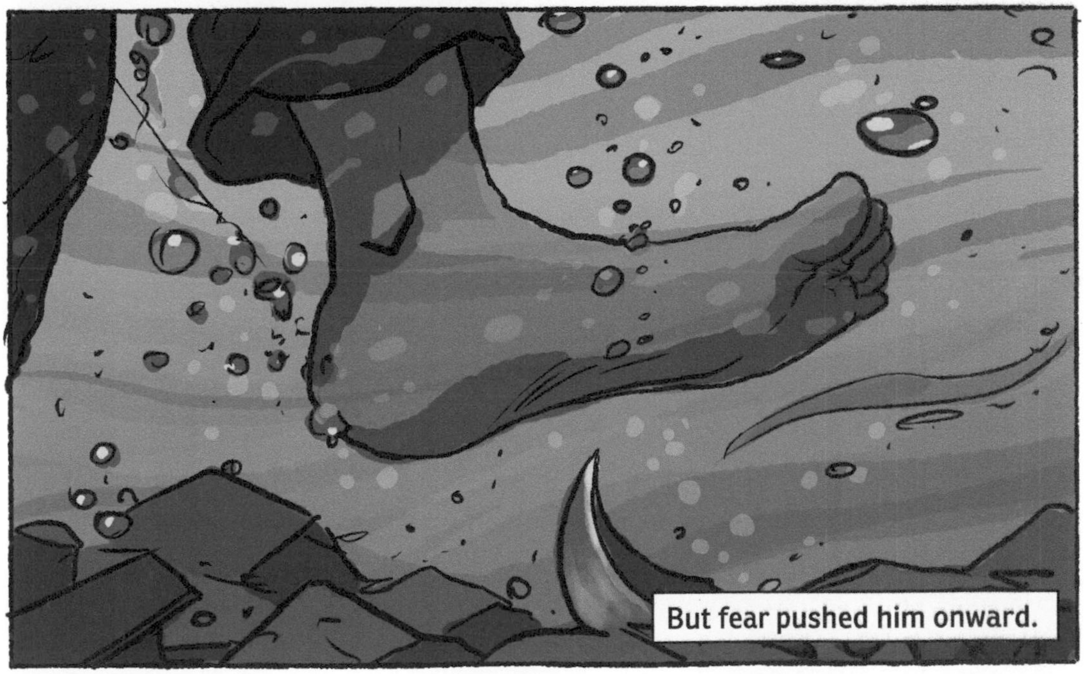
But fear pushed him onward.

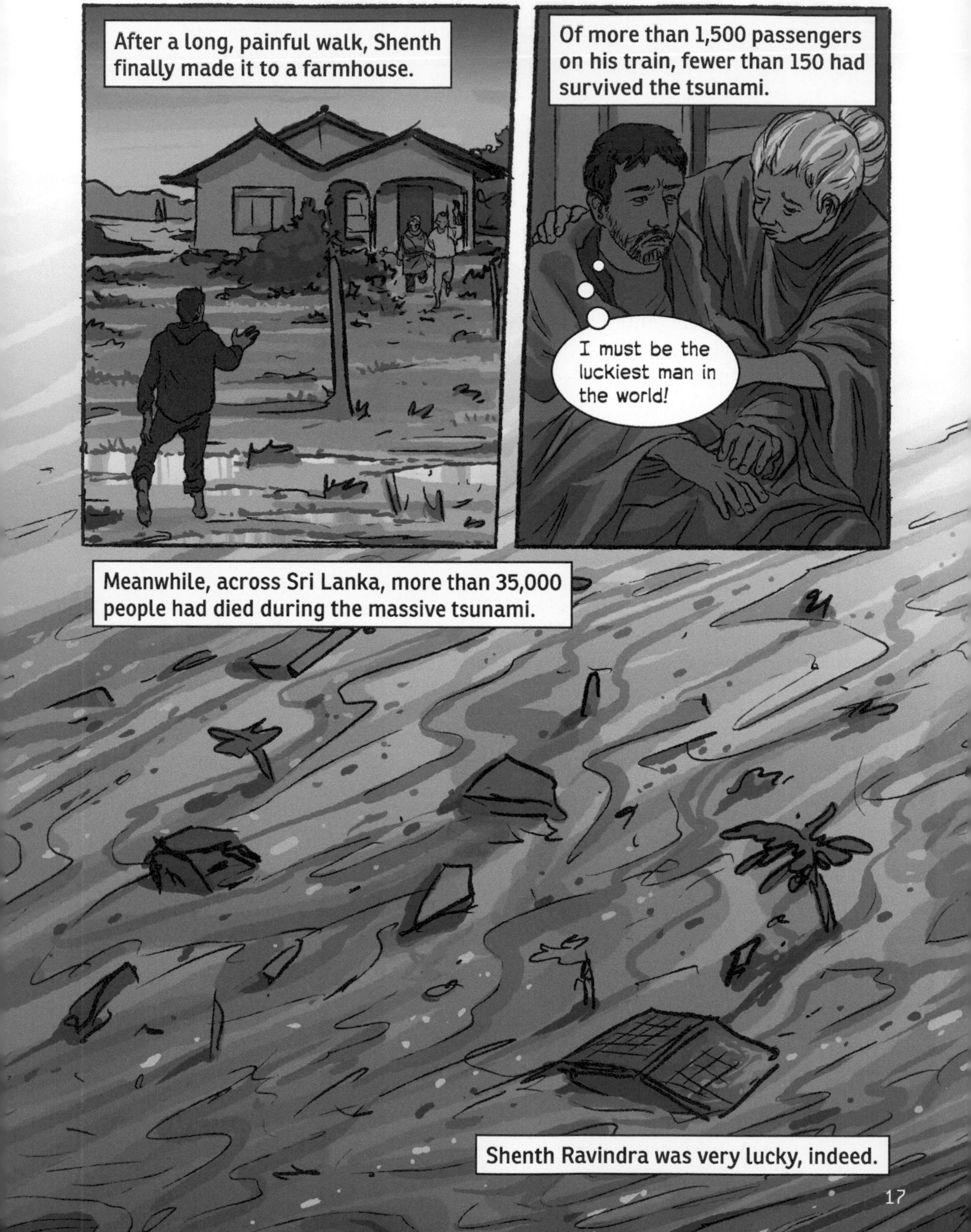
After a long, painful walk, Shenth finally made it to a farmhouse.
Of more than 1,500 passengers on his train, fewer than 150 had survived the tsunami.
I must be the luckiest man in the world!
Meanwhile, across Sri Lanka, more than 35,000 people had died during the massive tsunami.
Shenth Ravindra was very lucky, indeed.

CHAPTER 2

UNEXPECTED ERUPTION!

Mount Ontake sits nearly 125 miles (201 kilometers) west of Tokyo, Japan. It is the second-tallest volcano in the country.

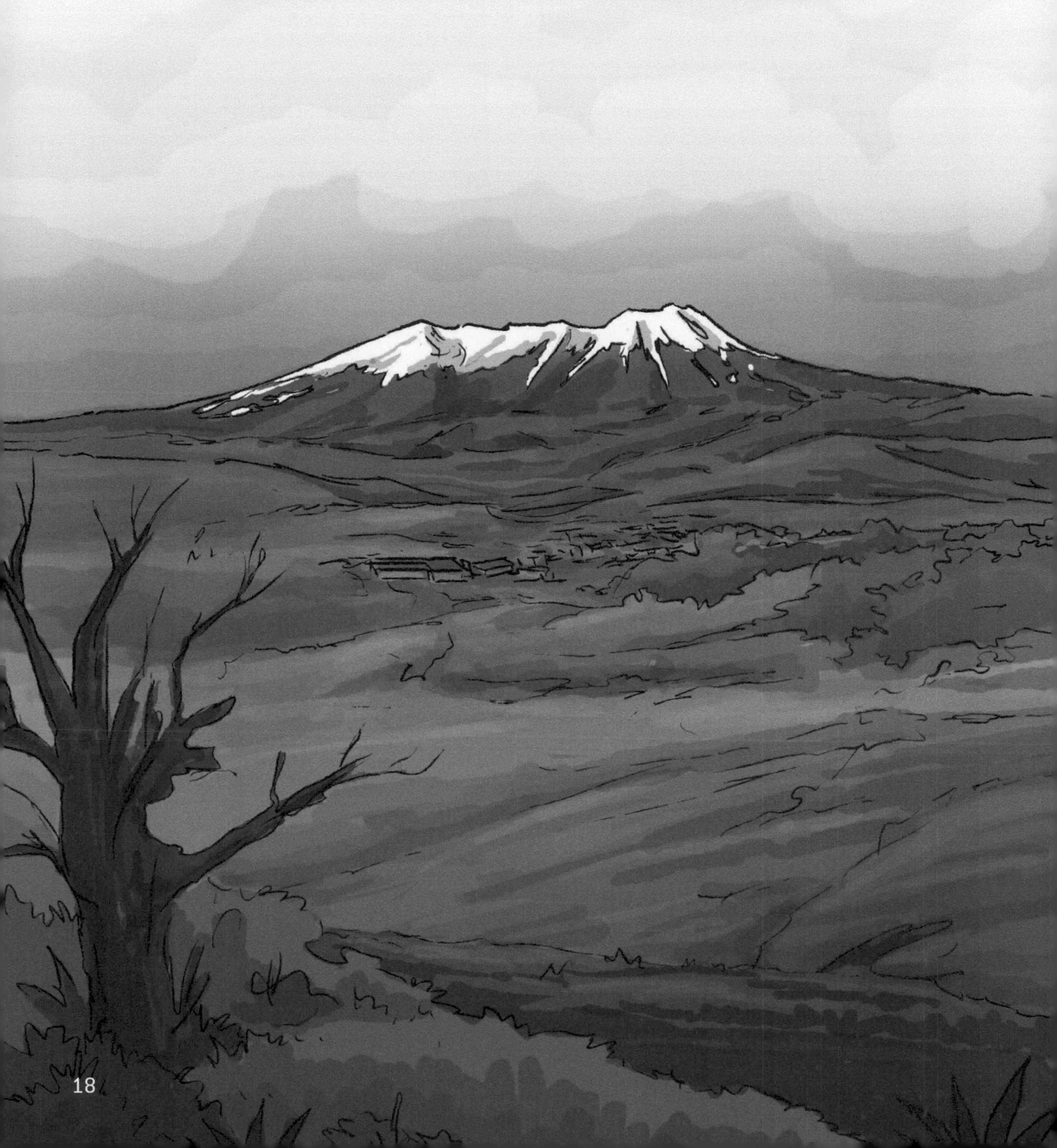

For many years, it sat silent and was a popular hiking spot.

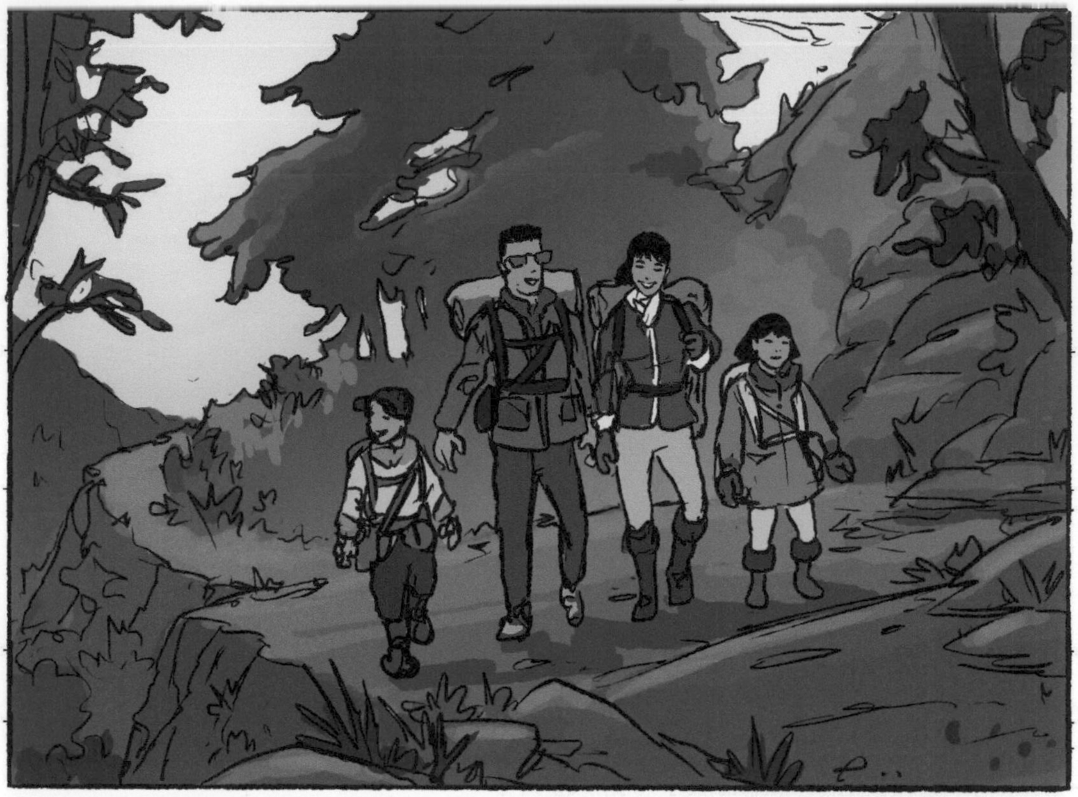

But on September 27, 2014, everything changed.

The mountain was full of visitors. And 63 of them would never leave it alive.

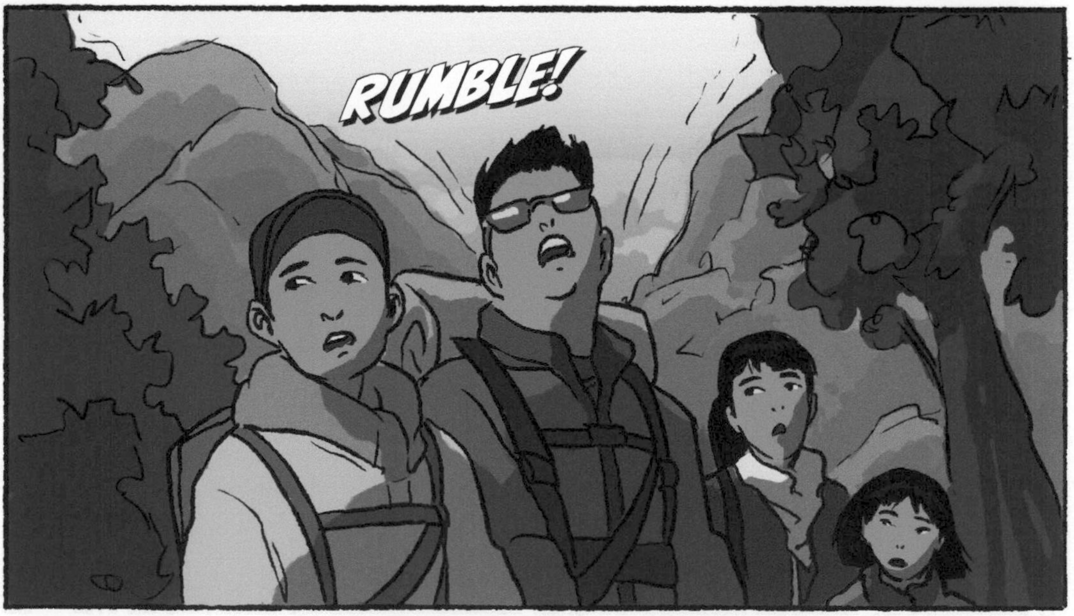
RUMBLE!

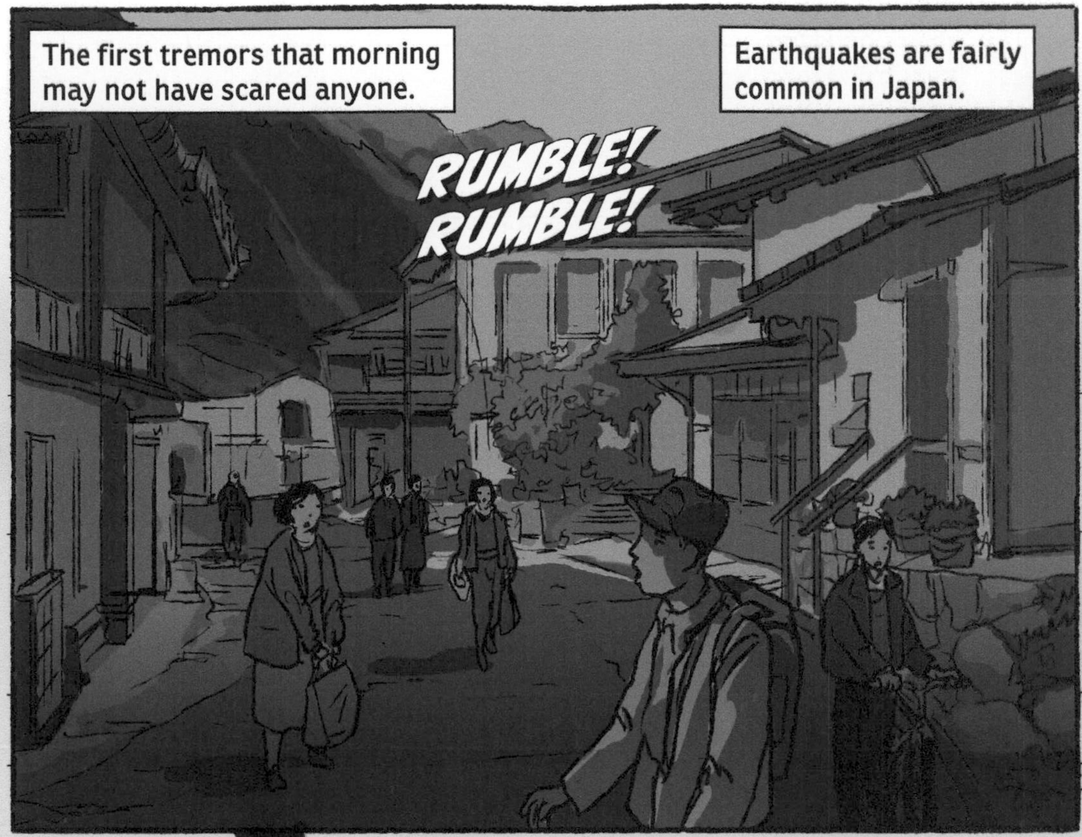
The first tremors that morning may not have scared anyone.
Earthquakes are fairly common in Japan.
RUMBLE! RUMBLE!

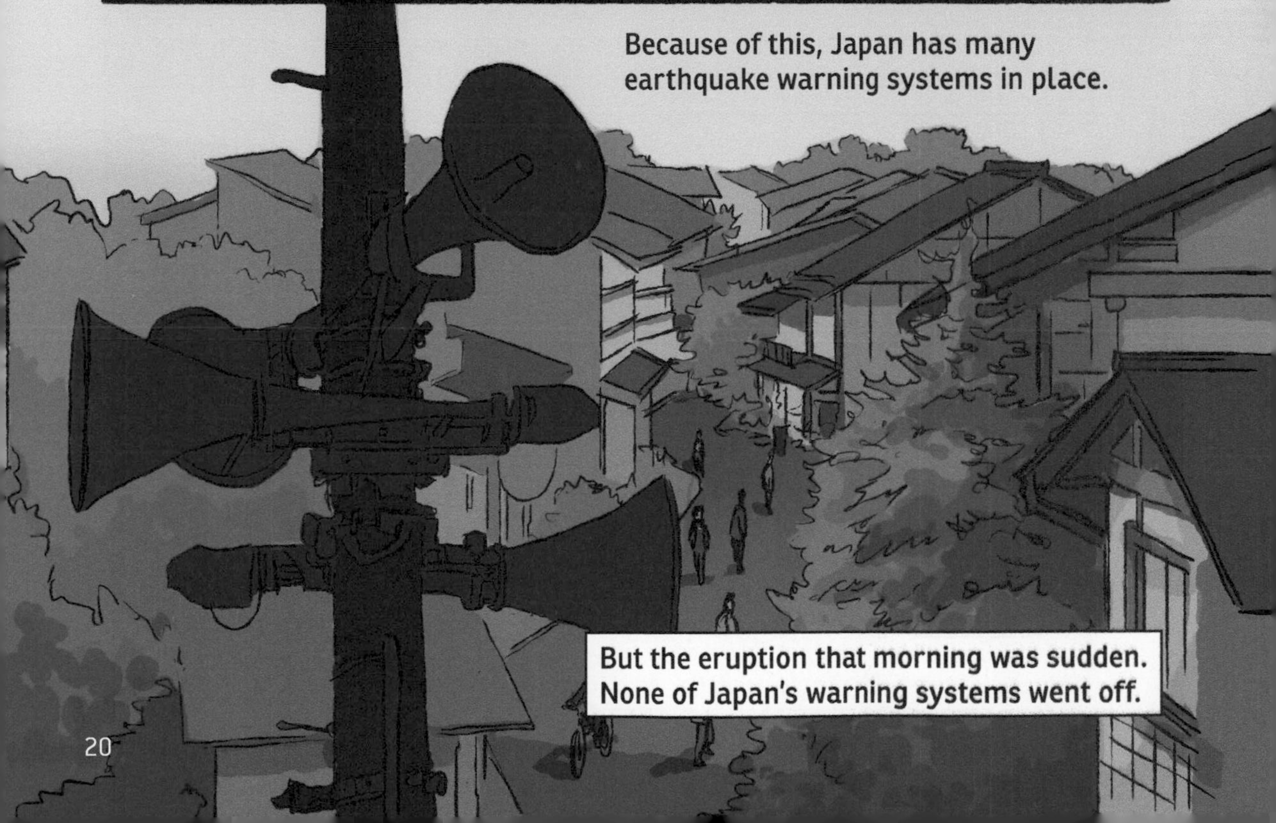
Because of this, Japan has many earthquake warning systems in place.
But the eruption that morning was sudden. None of Japan's warning systems went off.

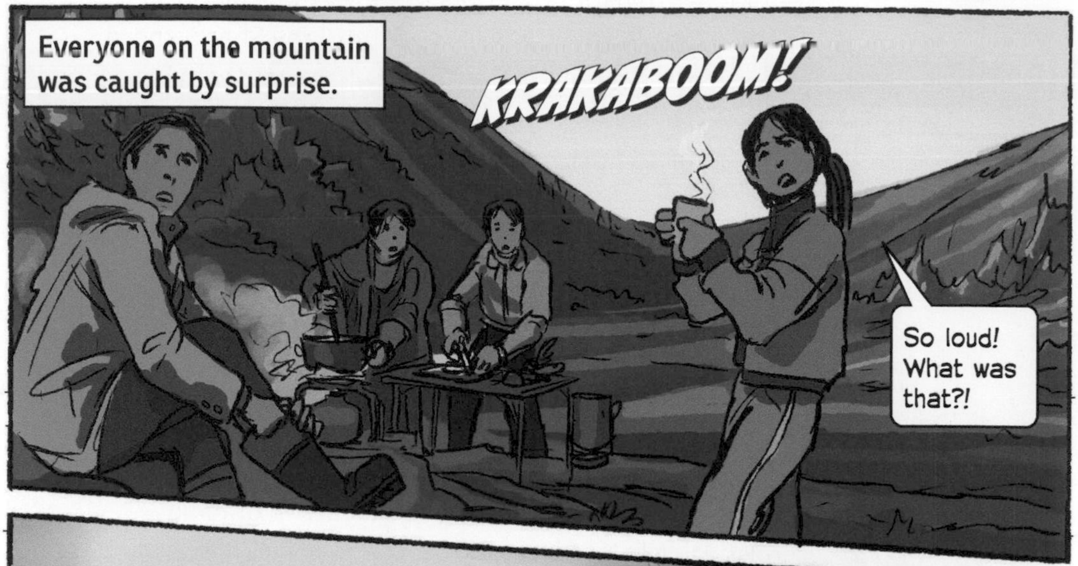
Everyone on the mountain
was caught by surprise.
KRAKABOOM!
So loud! What was that?!

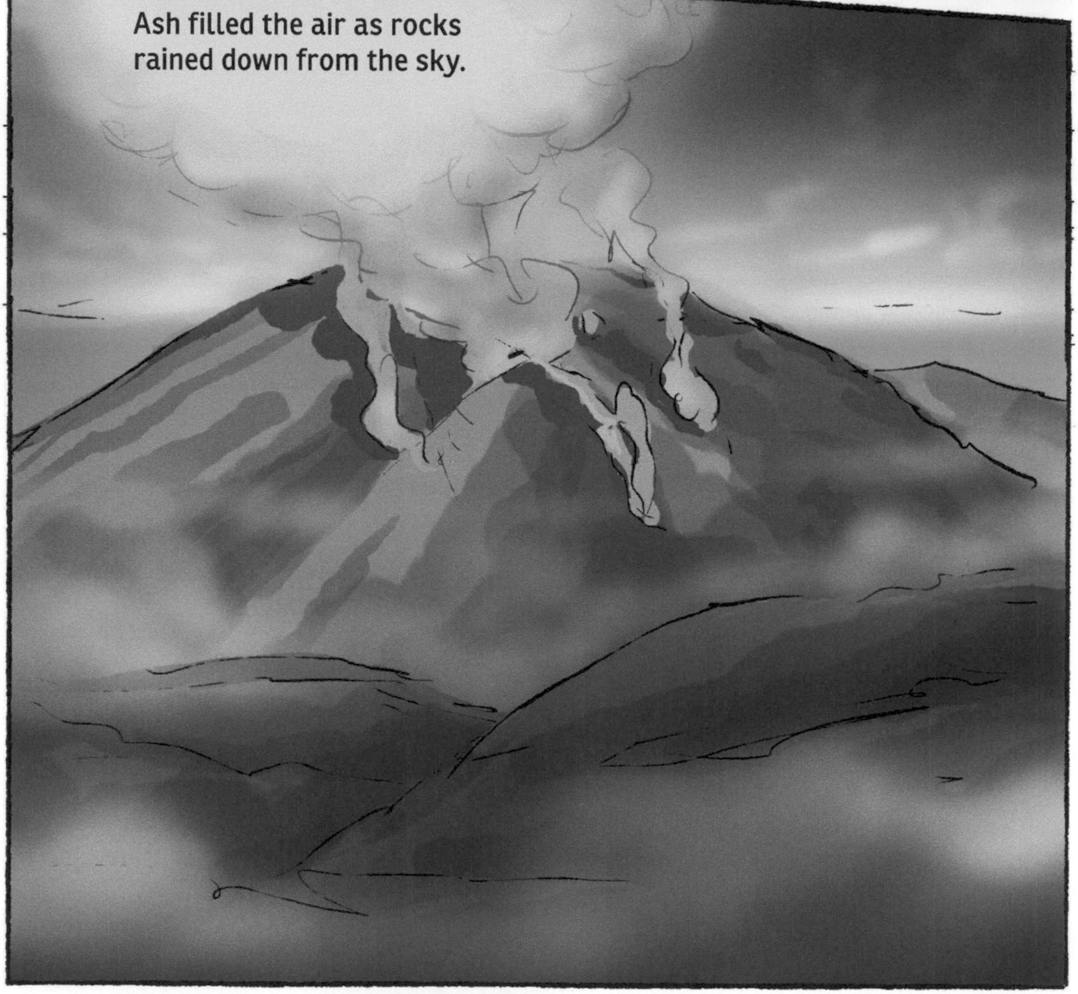
Ash filled the air as rocks
rained down from the sky.

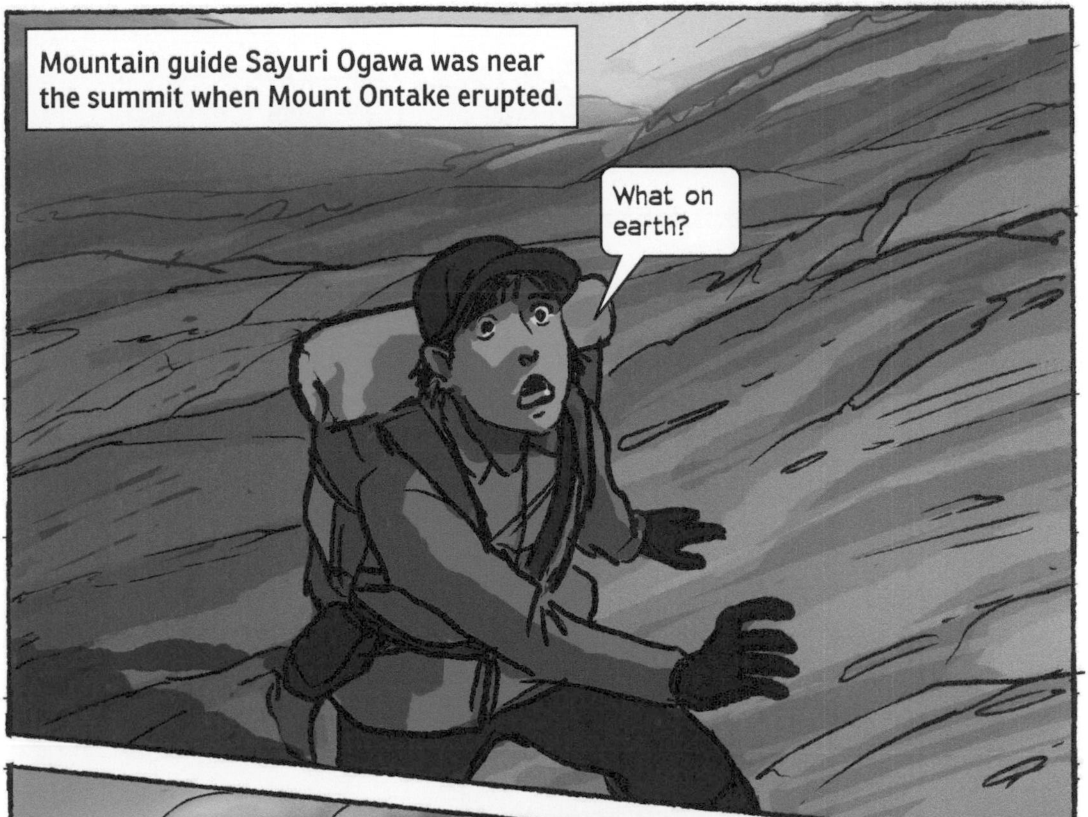
Mountain guide Sayuri Ogawa was near the summit when Mount Ontake erupted.
What on earth?

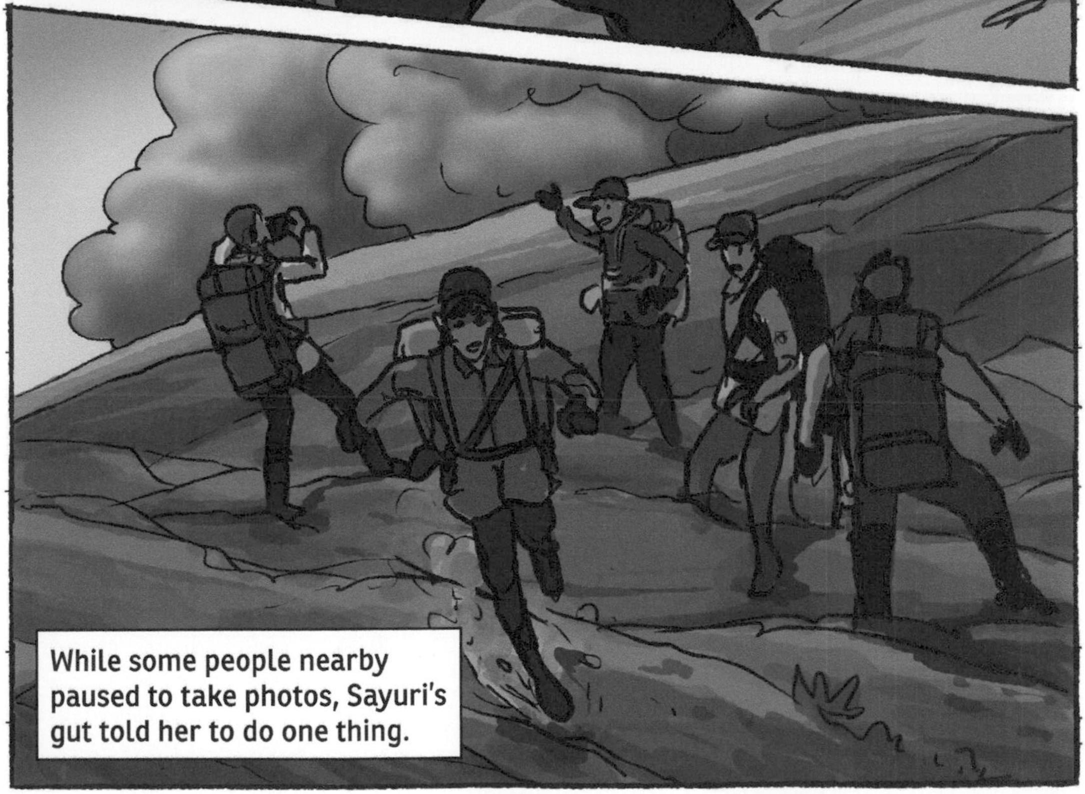
While some people nearby paused to take photos, Sayuri's gut told her to do one thing.

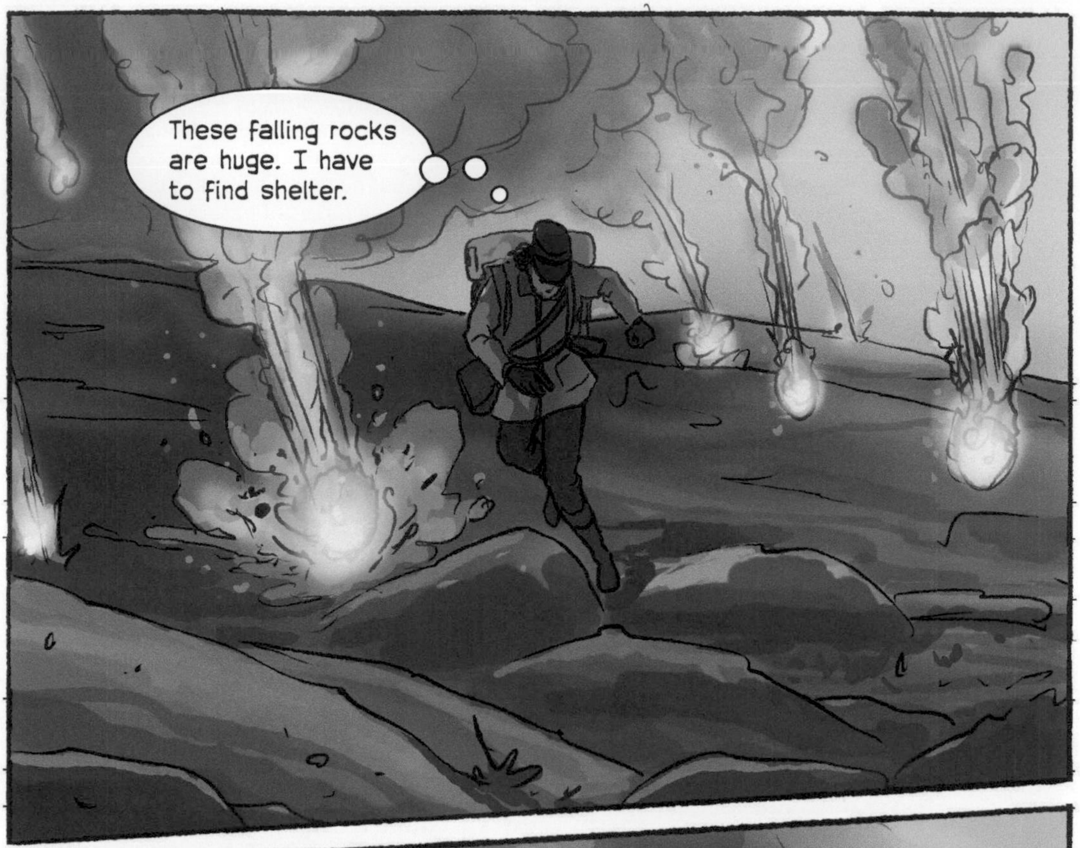
These falling rocks are huge. I have to find shelter.

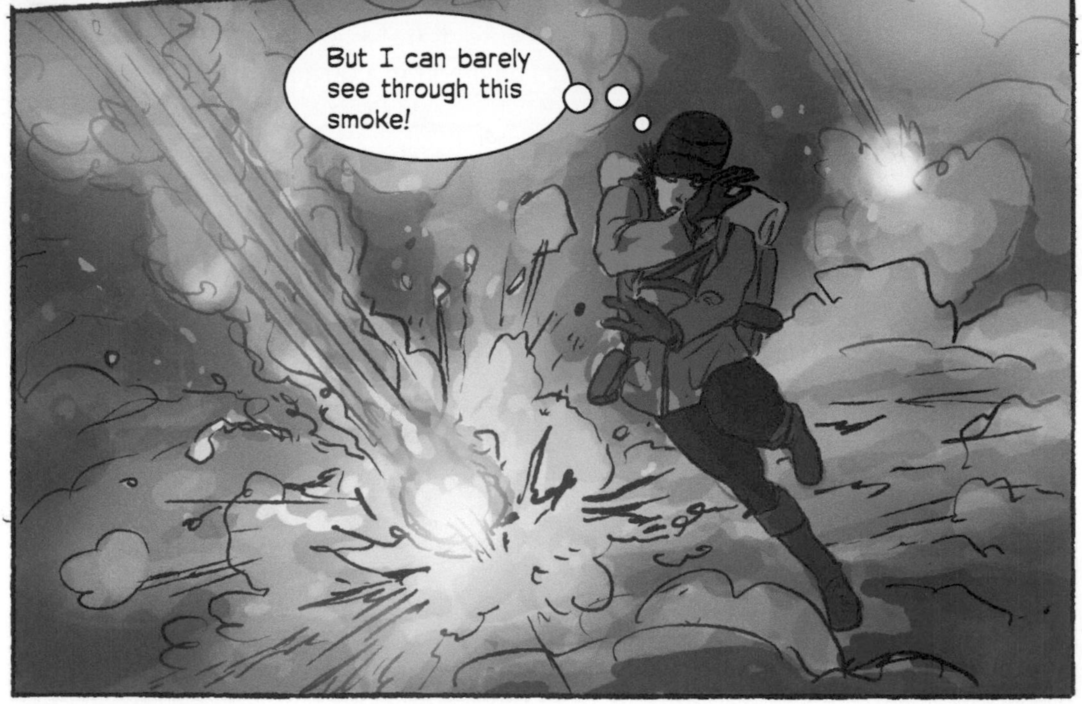
But I can barely see through this smoke!

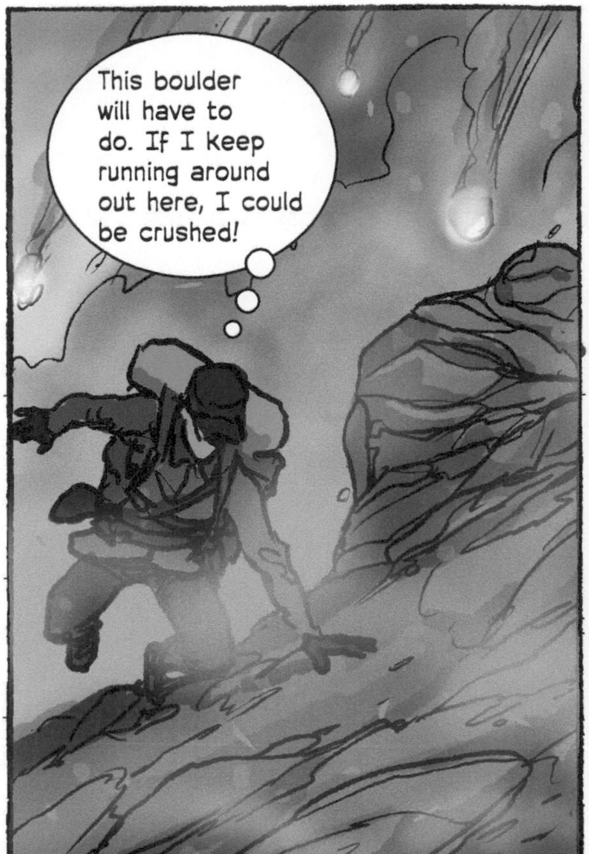
This boulder will have to do. If I keep running around out here, I could be crushed!

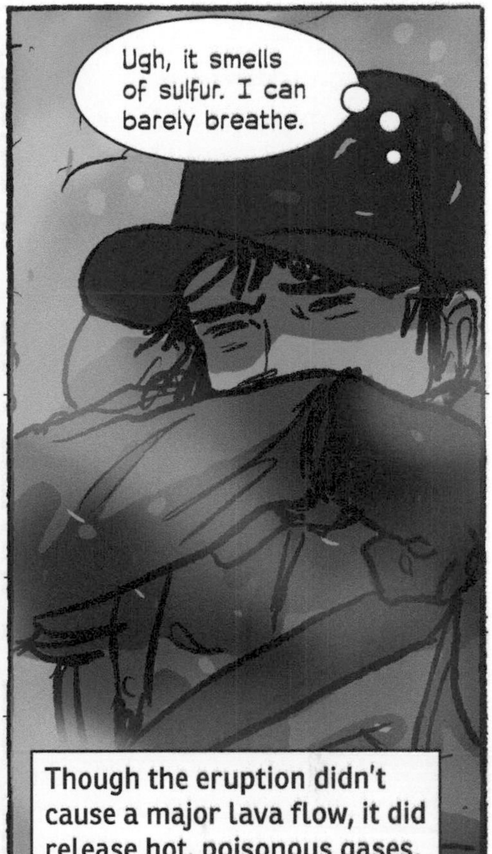
Ugh, it smells of sulfur. I can barely breathe.
Though the eruption didn't cause a major lava flow, it did release hot, poisonous gases.

When the air cleared for a moment, Sayuri dashed for a larger rock formation.

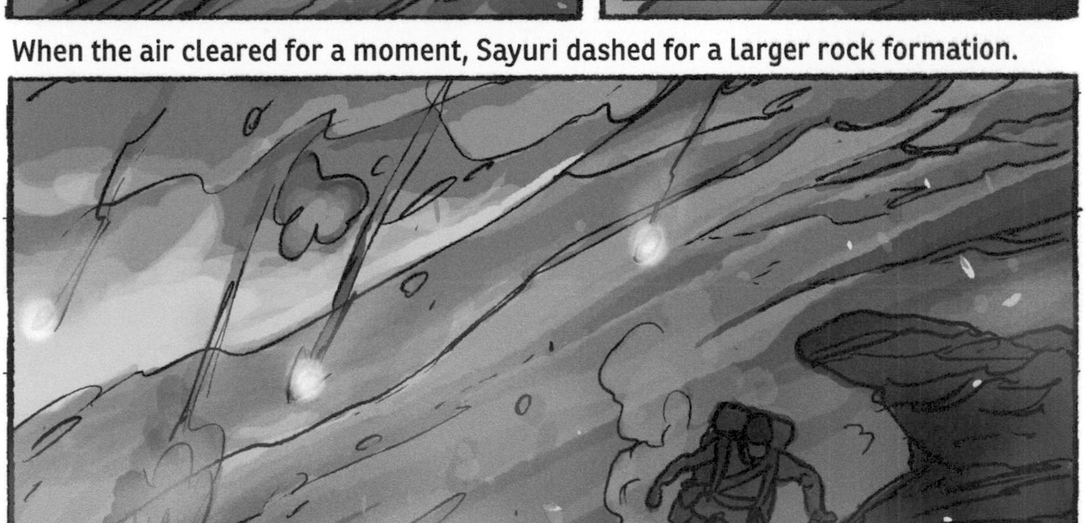

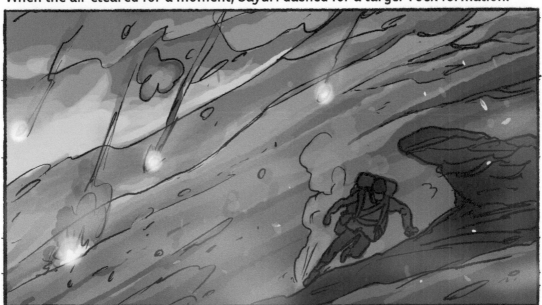

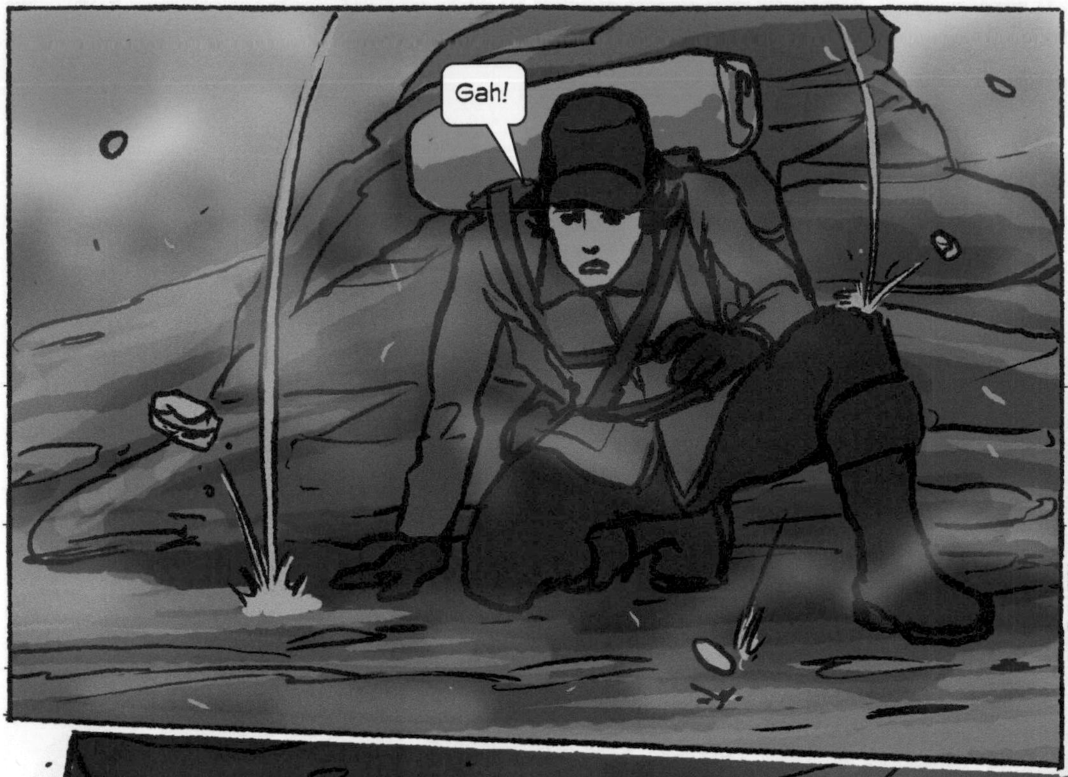
Gah!

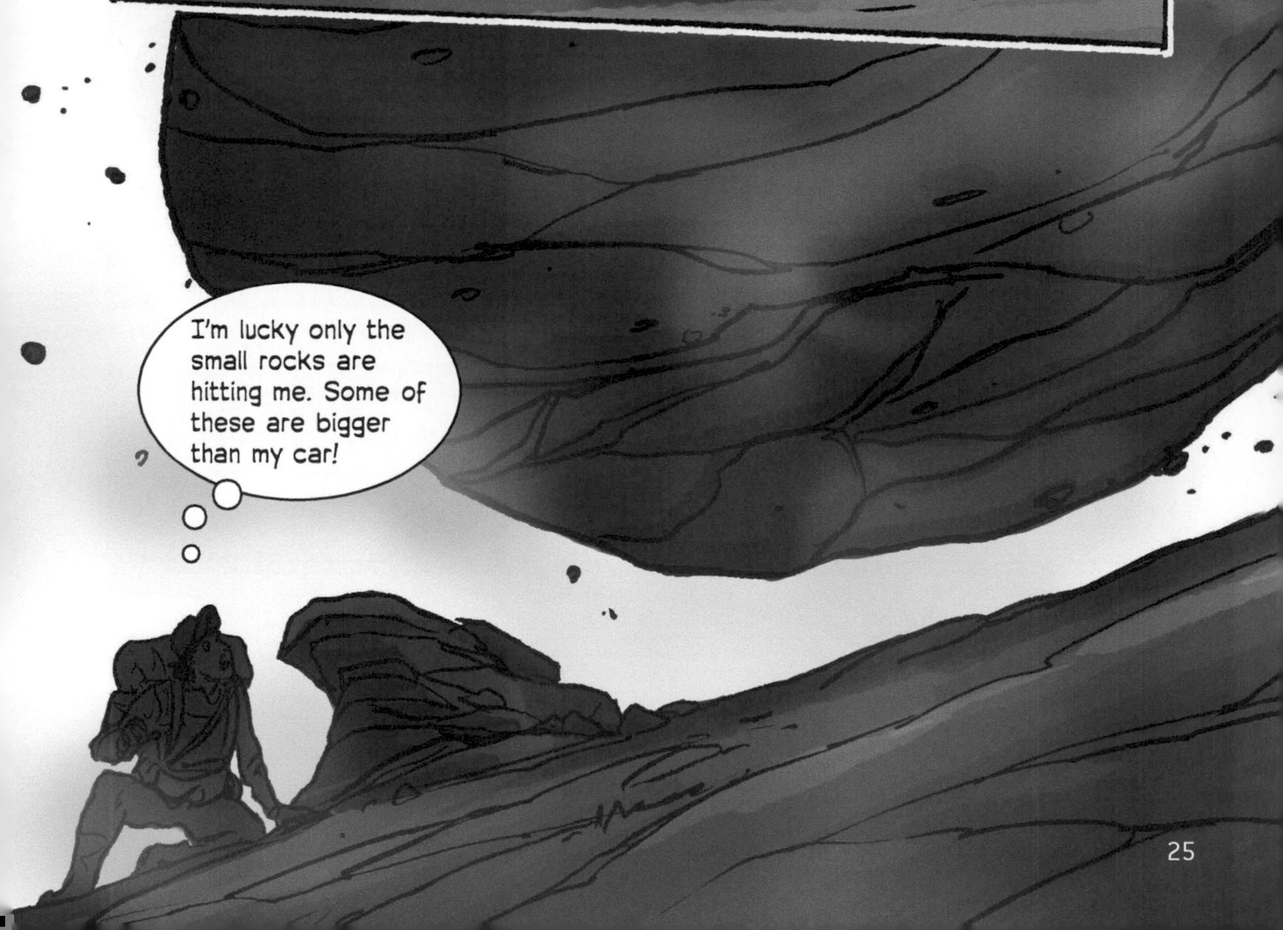
I'm lucky only the small rocks are hitting me. Some of these are bigger than my car!

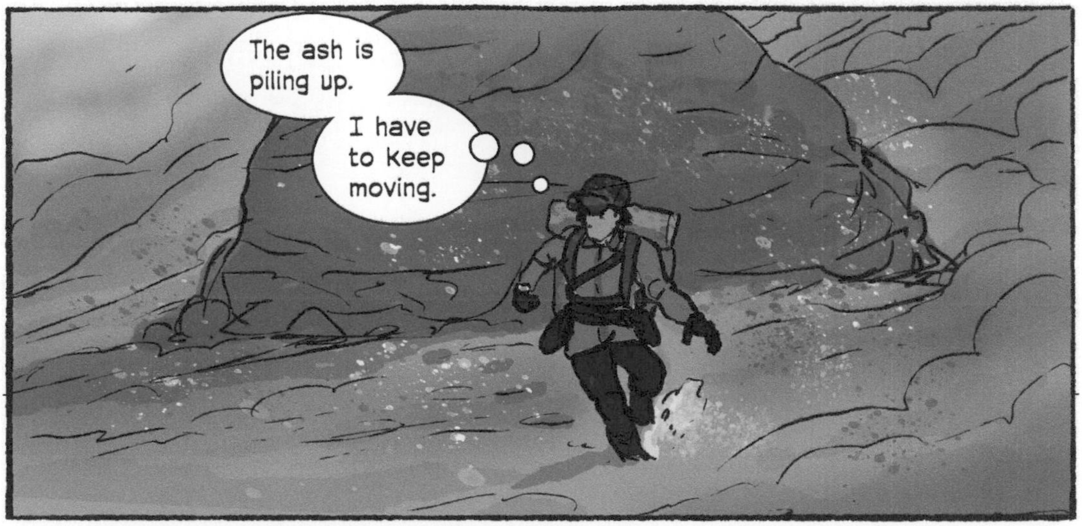
The ash is piling up.
I have to keep moving.

Eventually, Sayuri reached a mountain lodge.

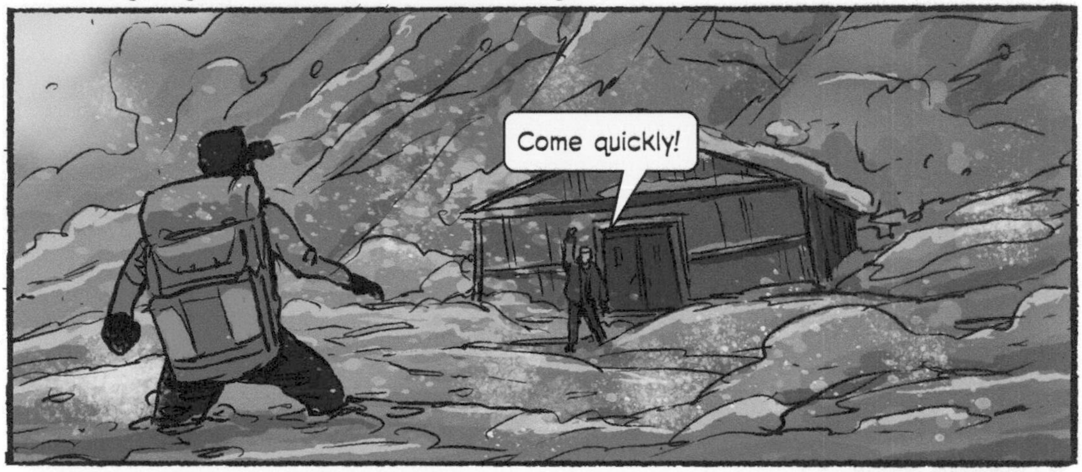
Come quickly!

Inside, she saw dozens of survivors.

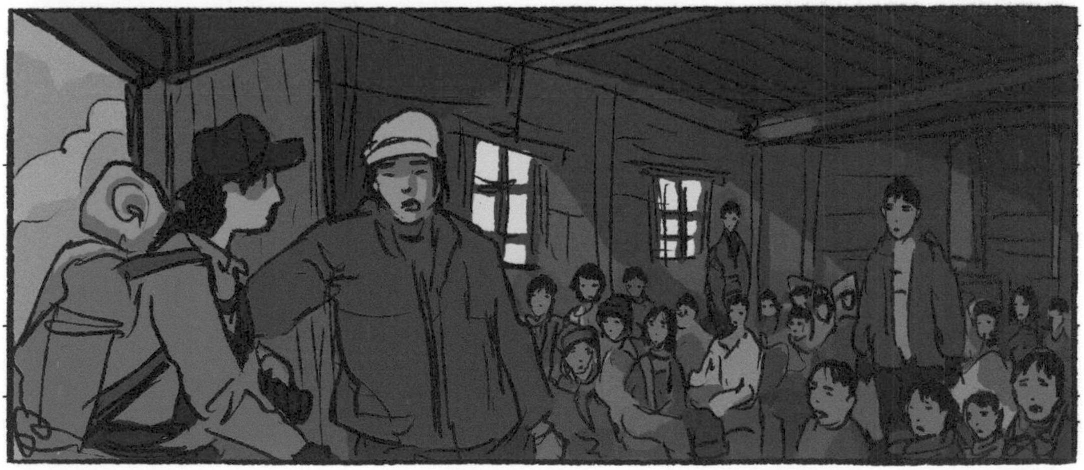

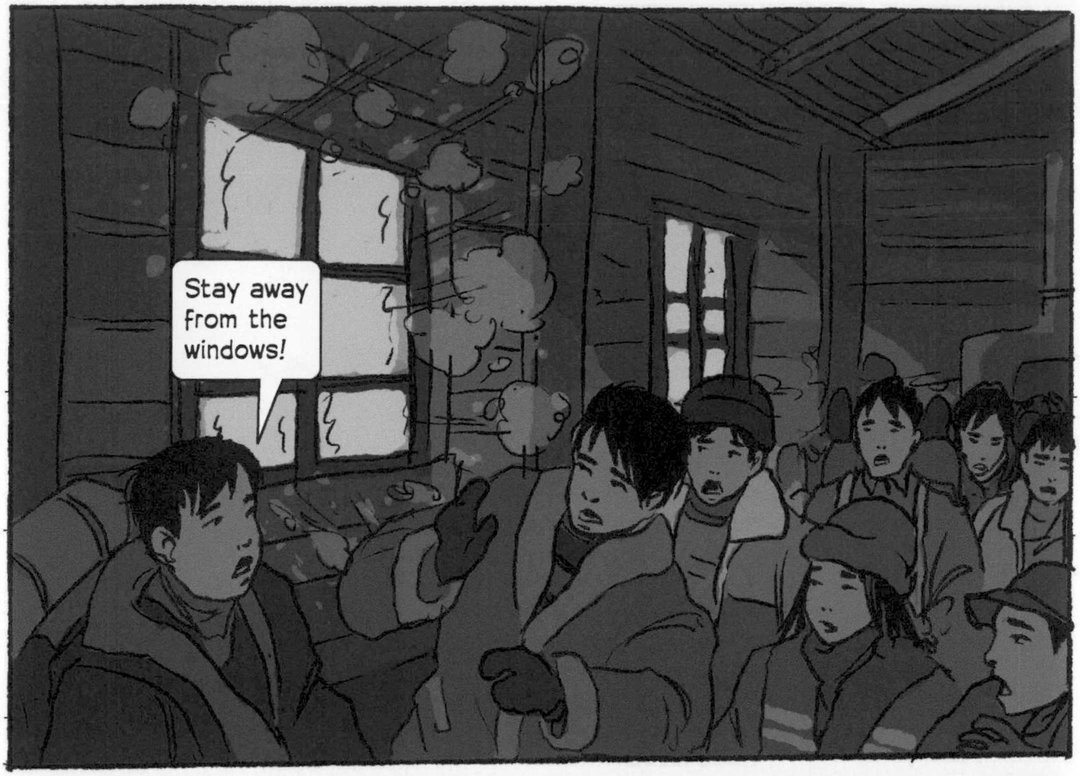
Stay away from the windows!

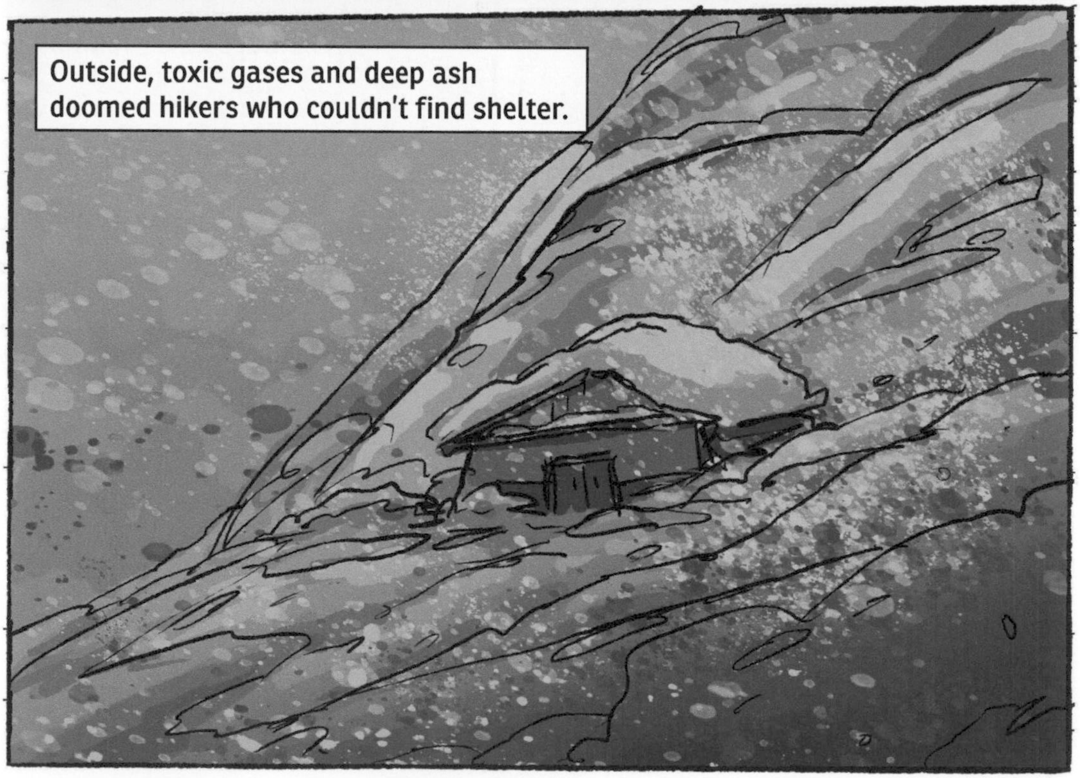
Outside, toxic gases and deep ash doomed hikers who couldn't find shelter.

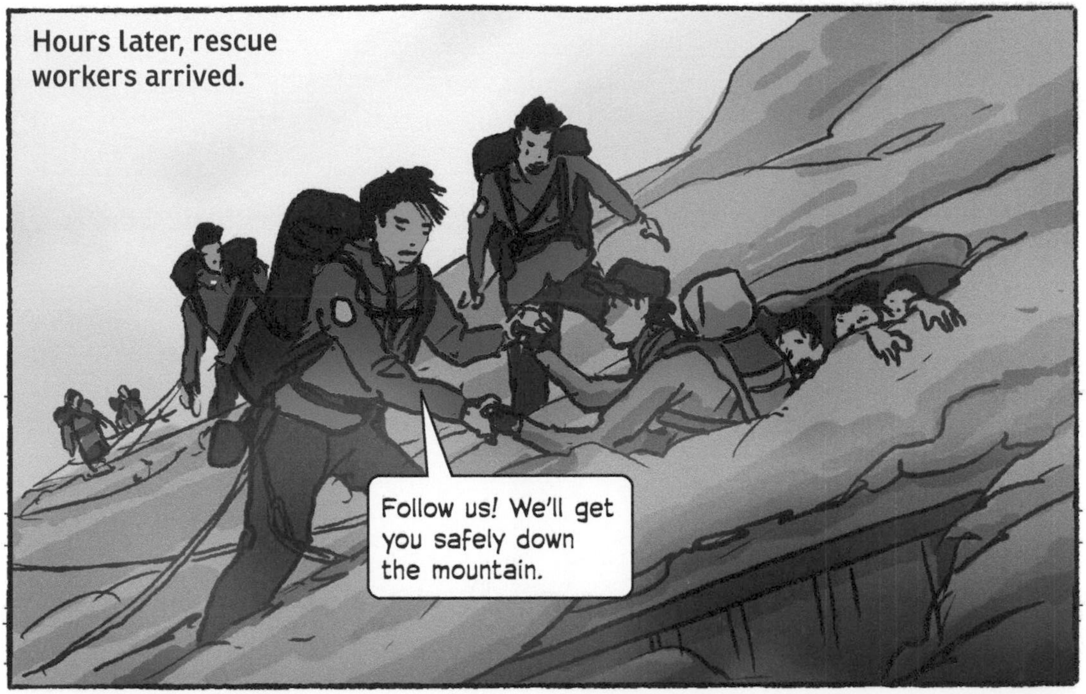
Hours later, rescue workers arrived.
Follow us! We'll get you safely down the mountain.

Rescue crews looked for missing people for more than a week.

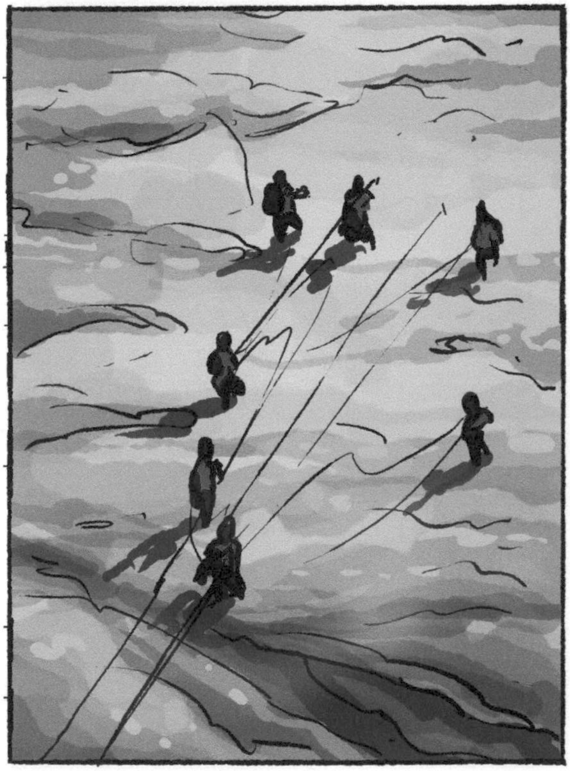

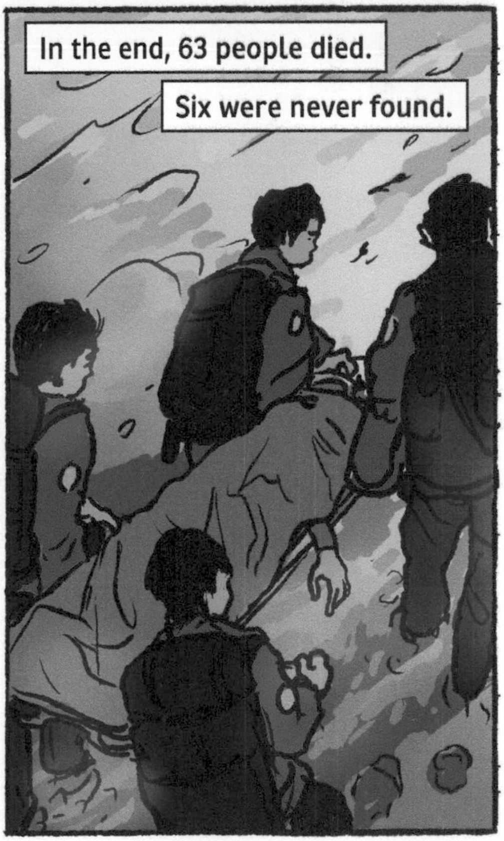
In the end, 63 people died.
Six were never found.

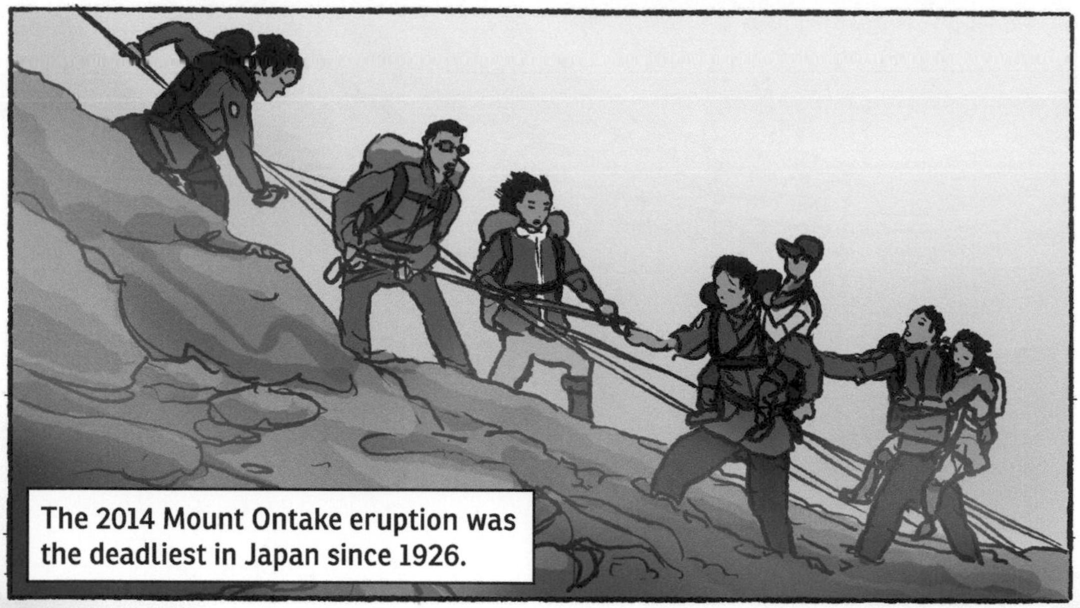
The 2014 Mount Ontake eruption was the deadliest in Japan since 1926.

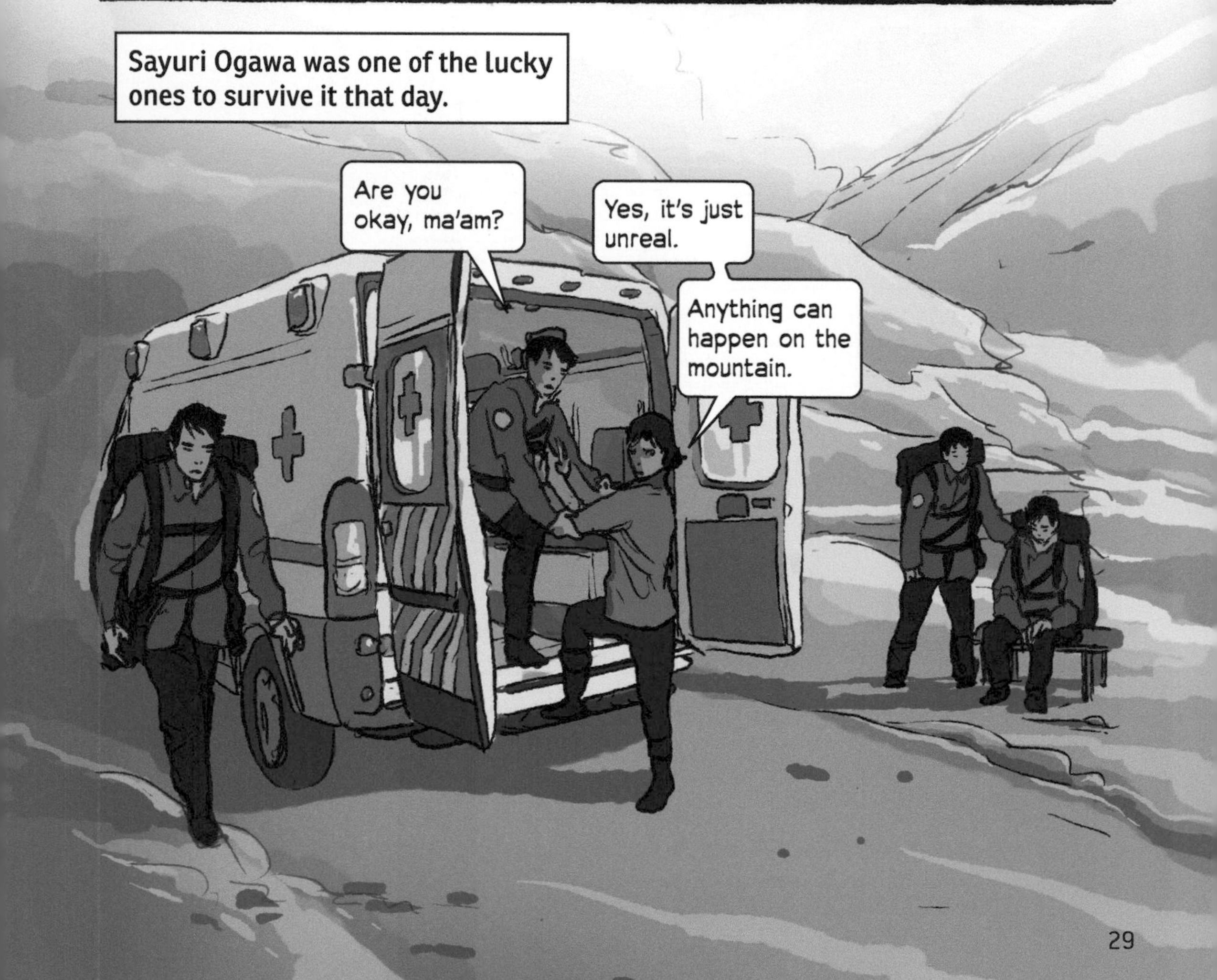
Sayuri Ogawa was one of the lucky ones to survive it that day.
Are you okay, ma'am?
Yes, it's just unreal.
Anything can happen on the mountain.

CHAPTER 3
UNTAMED INFERNO!

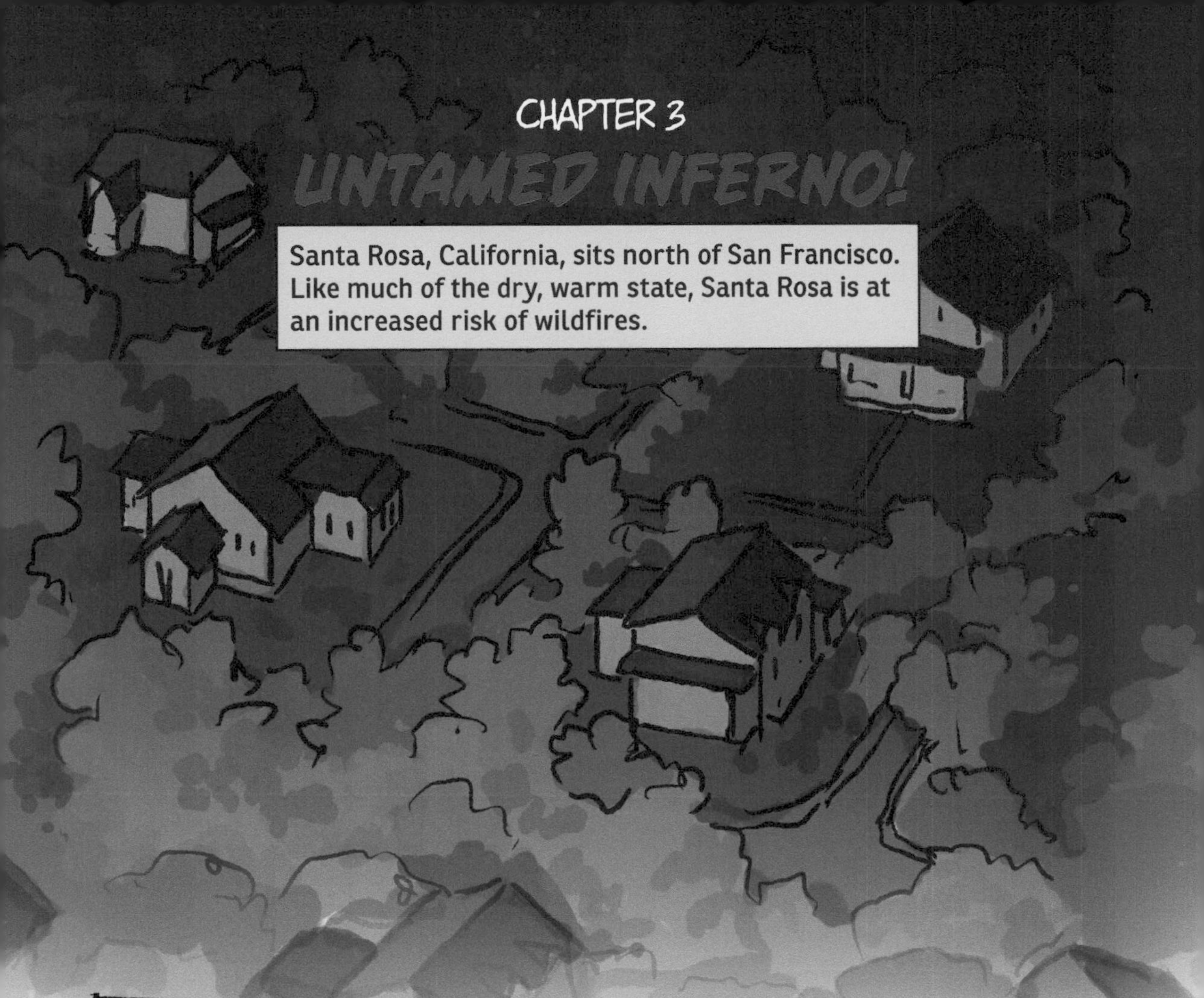
Santa Rosa, California, sits north of San Francisco. Like much of the dry, warm state, Santa Rosa is at an increased risk of wildfires.

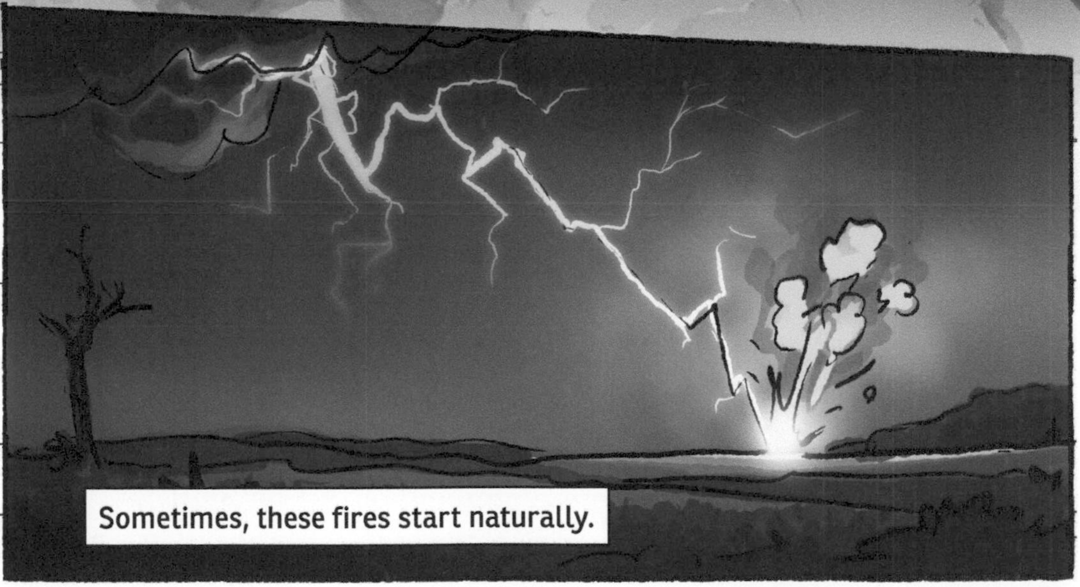
Sometimes, these fires start naturally.

Other times, people start them.

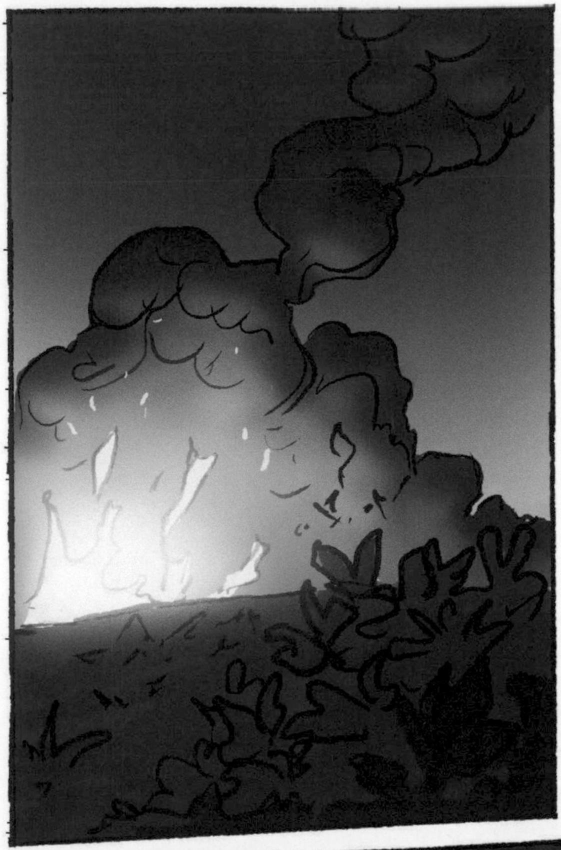

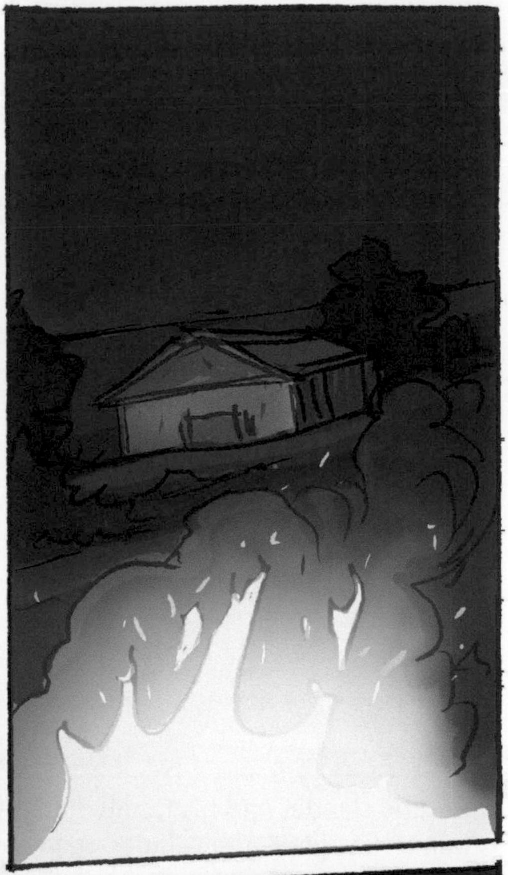

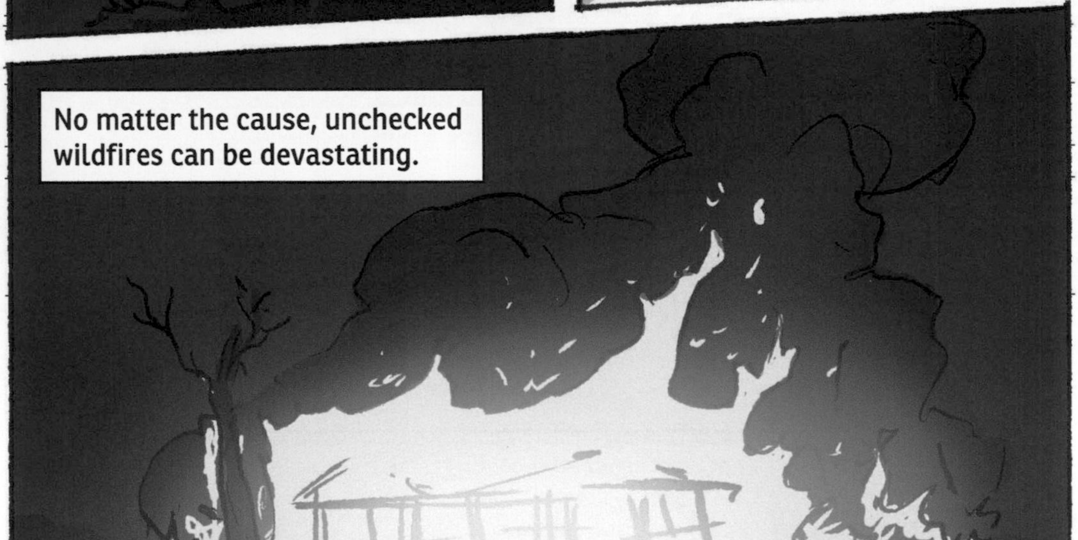
No matter the cause, unchecked wildfires can be devastating.

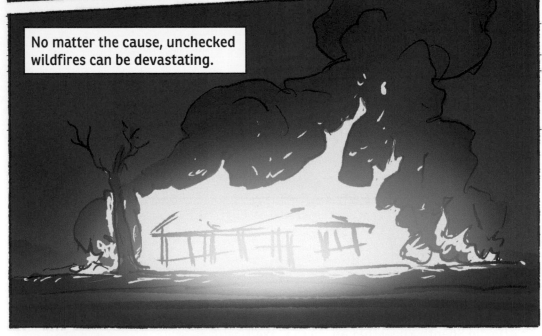

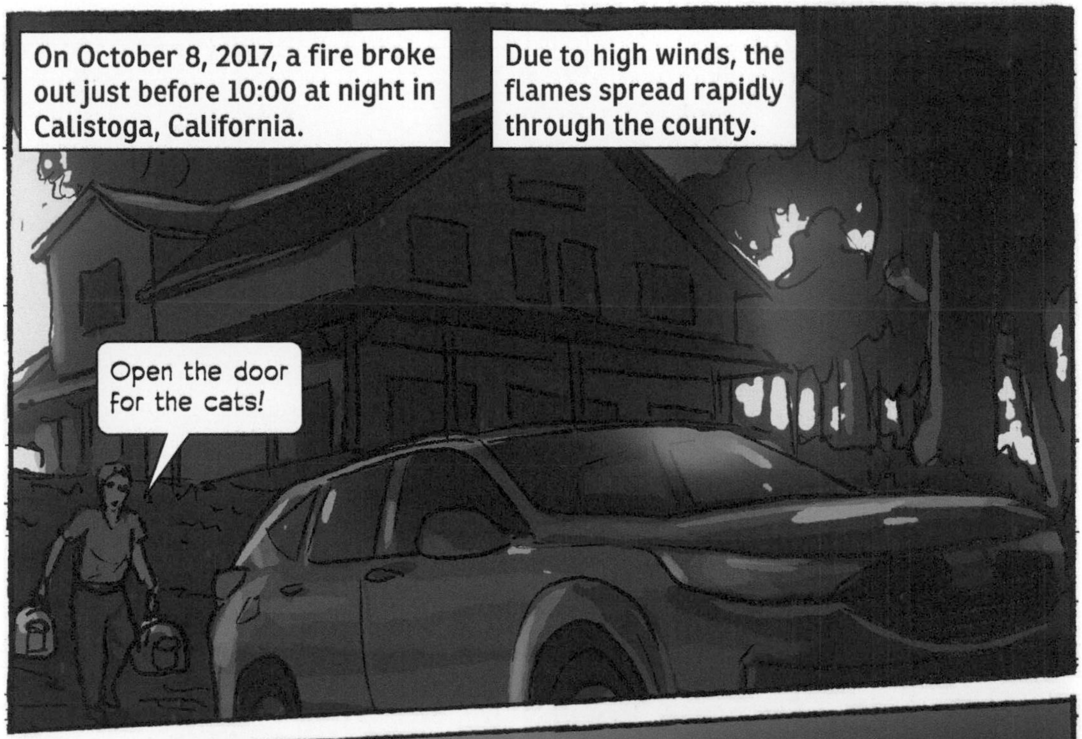
On October 8, 2017, a fire broke out just before 10:00 at night in Calistoga, California.
Due to high winds, the flames spread rapidly through the county.
Open the door for the cats!
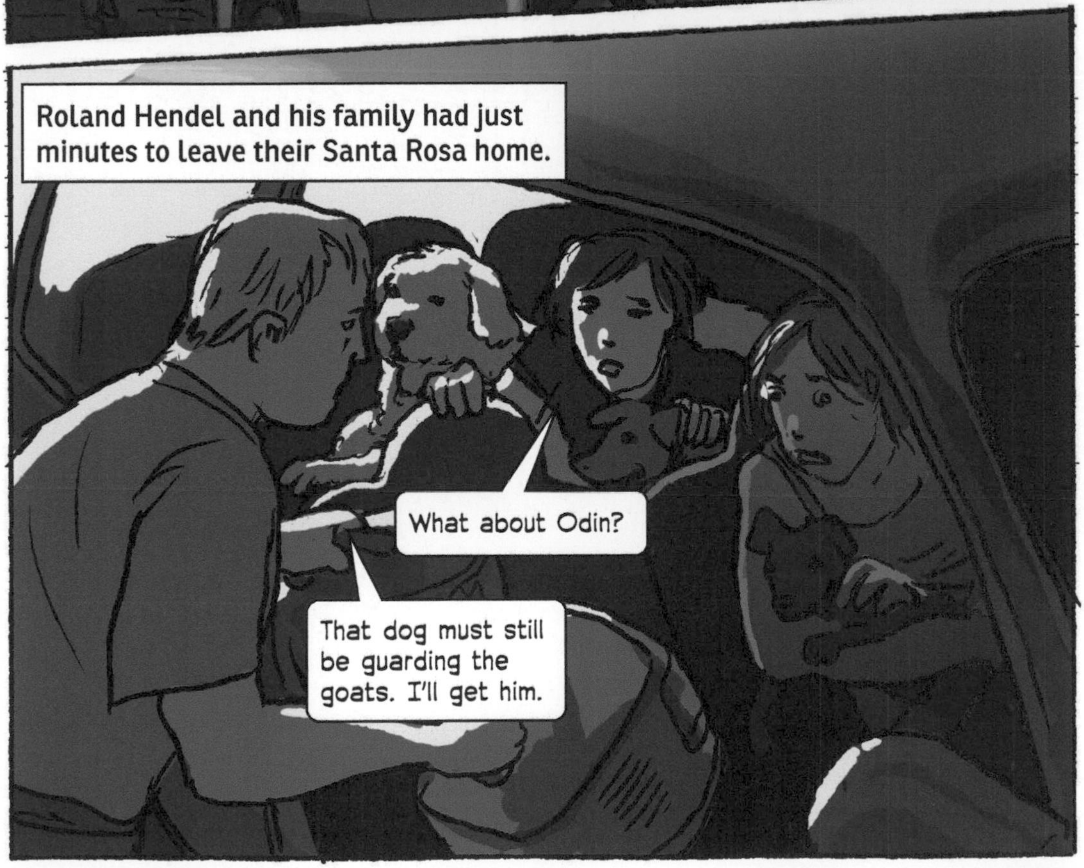
Roland Hendel and his family had just minutes to leave their Santa Rosa home.
What about Odin?
That dog must still be guarding the goats. I'll get him.

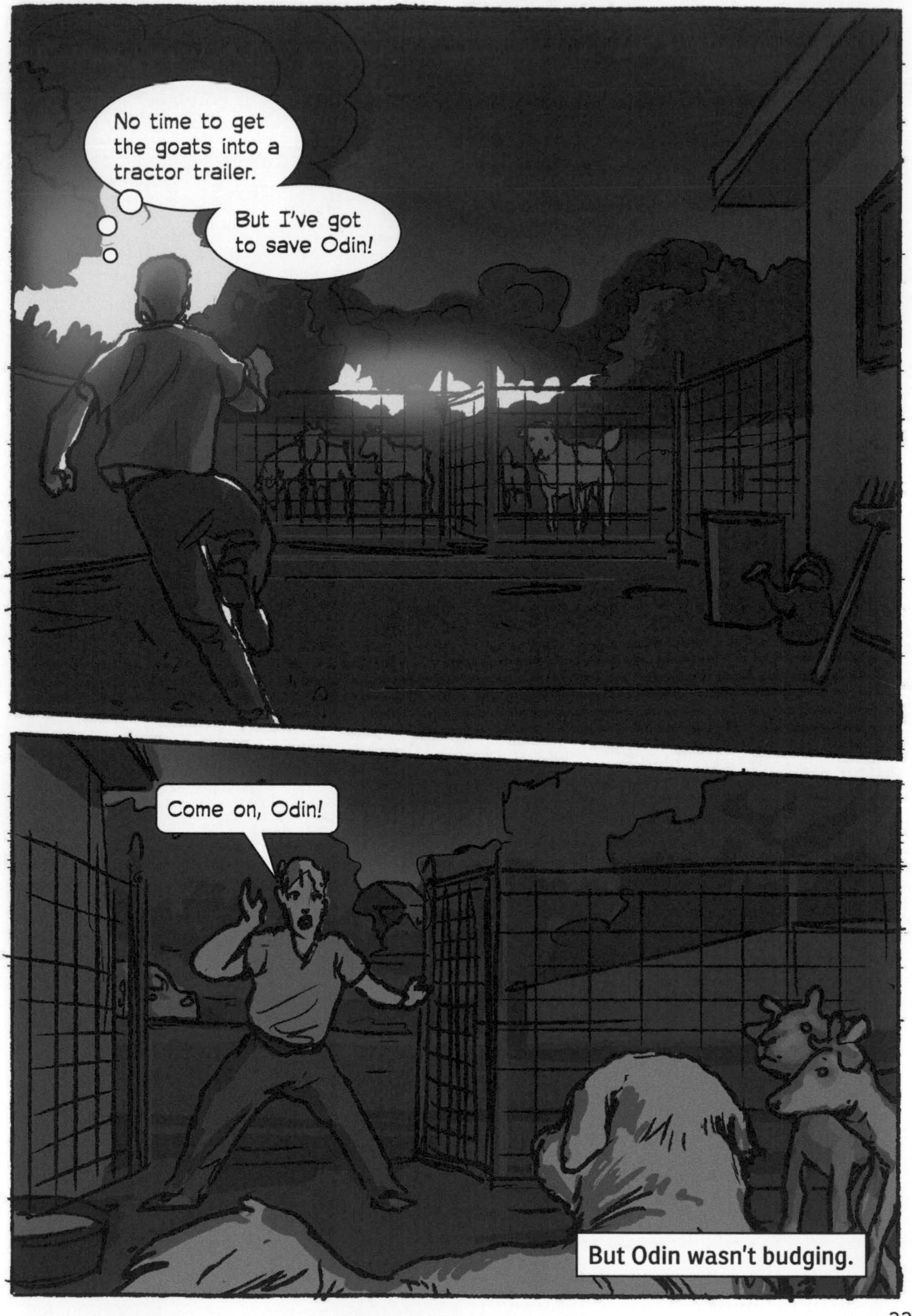
No time to get the goats into a tractor trailer.
But I've got to save Odin!
Come on, Odin!
But Odin wasn't budging.

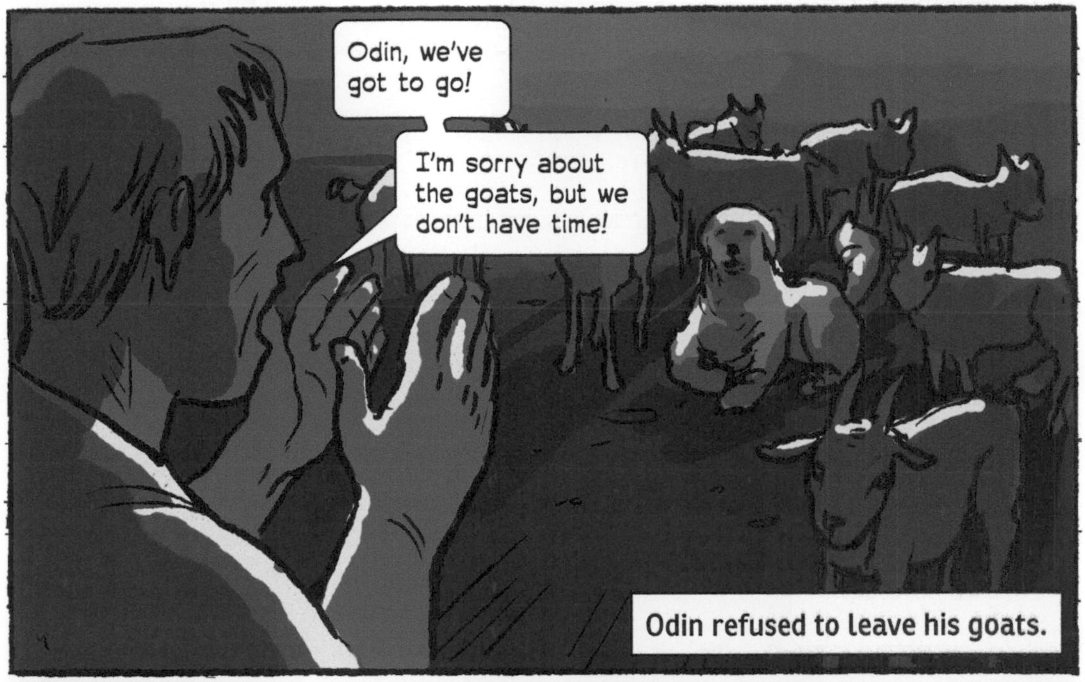
Odin, we've got to go!
I'm sorry about the goats, but we don't have time!
Odin refused to leave his goats.

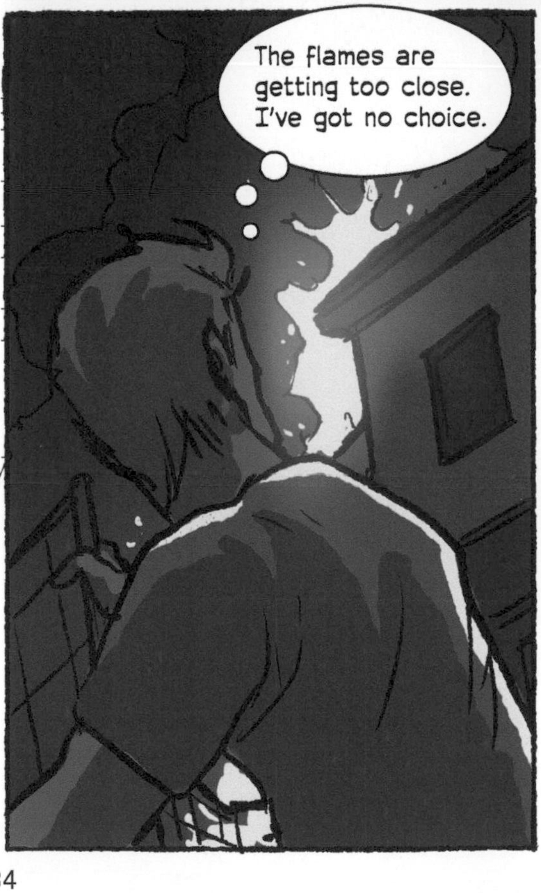
The flames are getting too close. I've got no choice.

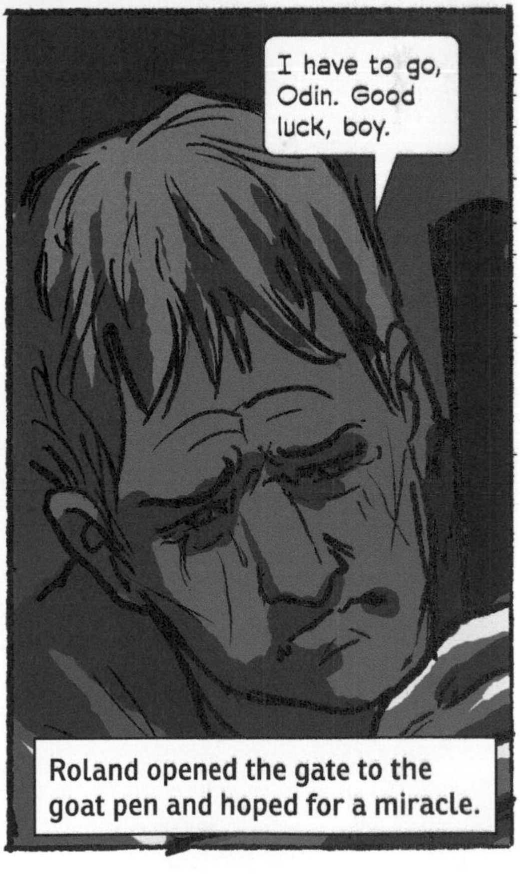
I have to go, Odin. Good luck, boy.
Roland opened the gate to the goat pen and hoped for a miracle.

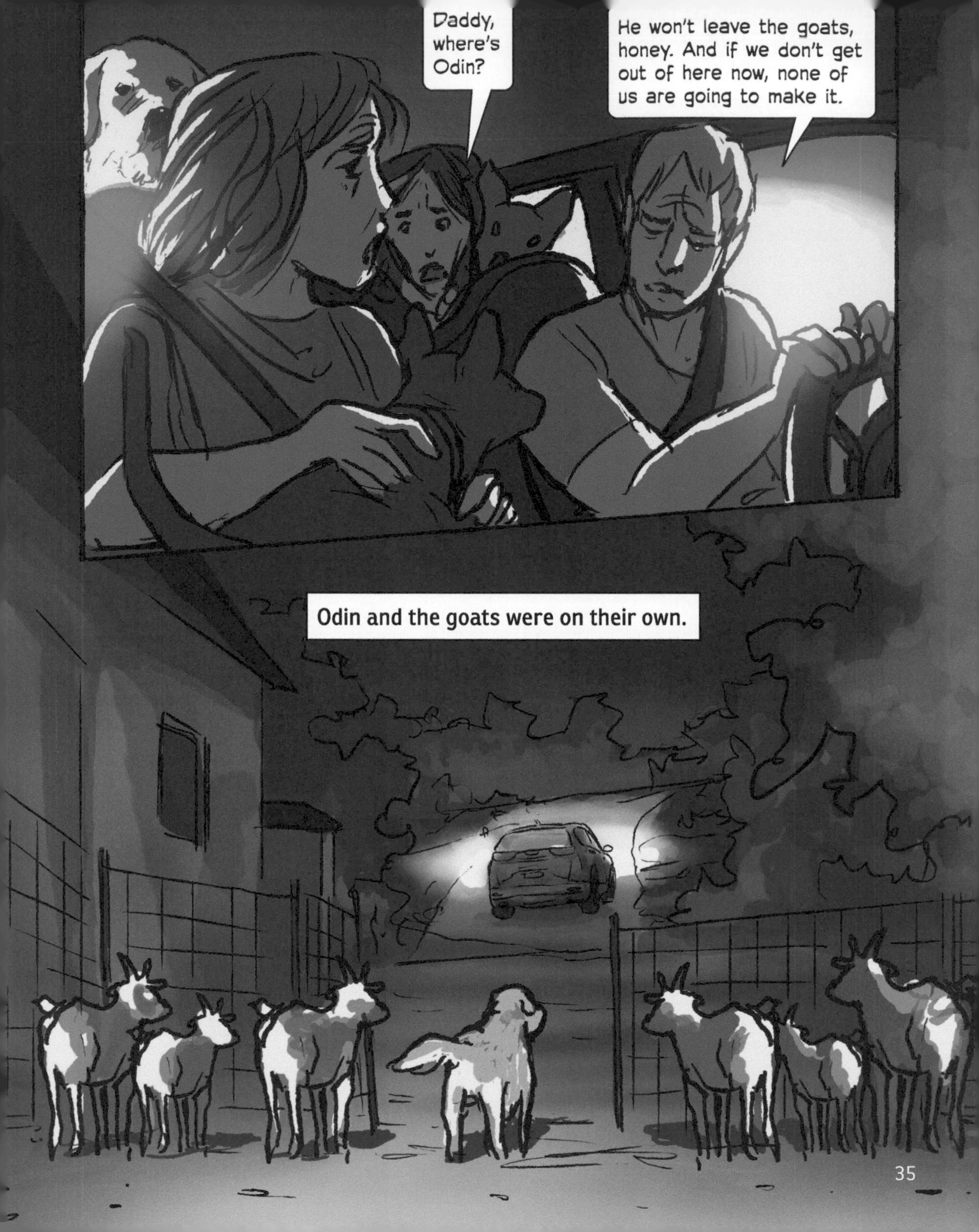
Daddy, where's Odin?
He won't leave the goats, honey. And if we don't get out of here now, none of us are going to make it.
Odin and the goats were on their own.

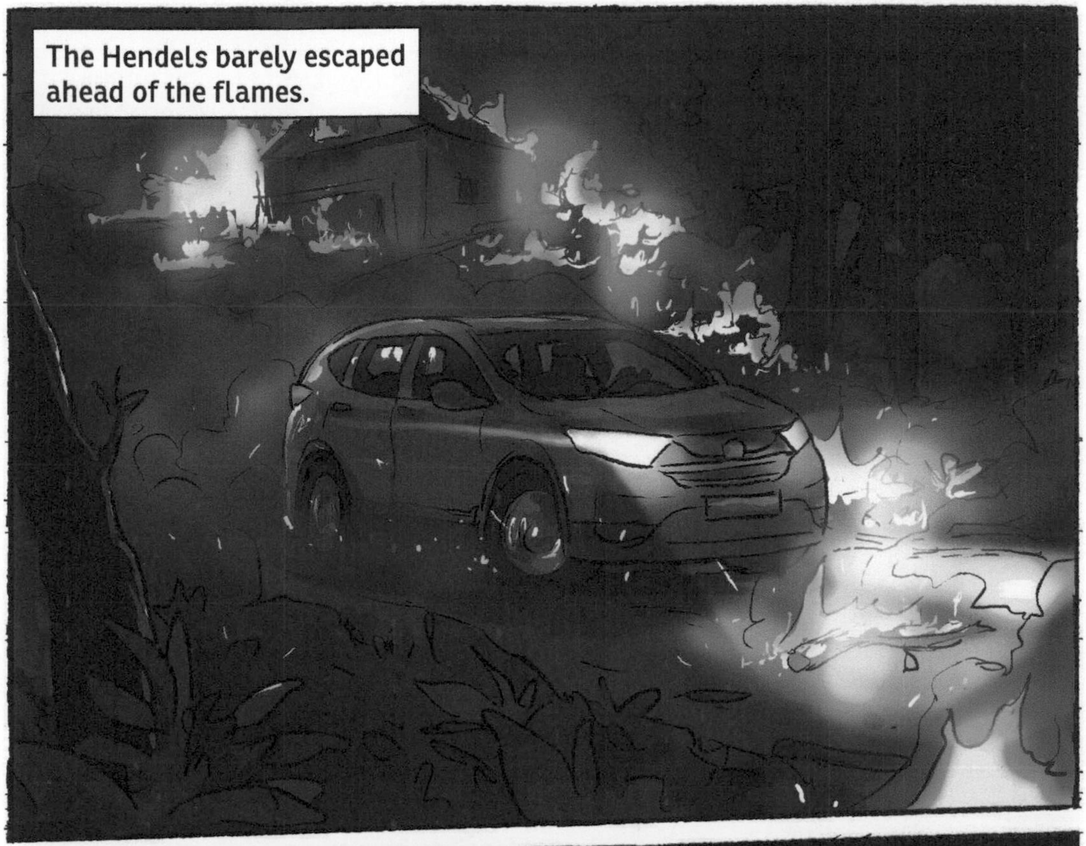
The Hendels barely escaped ahead of the flames.

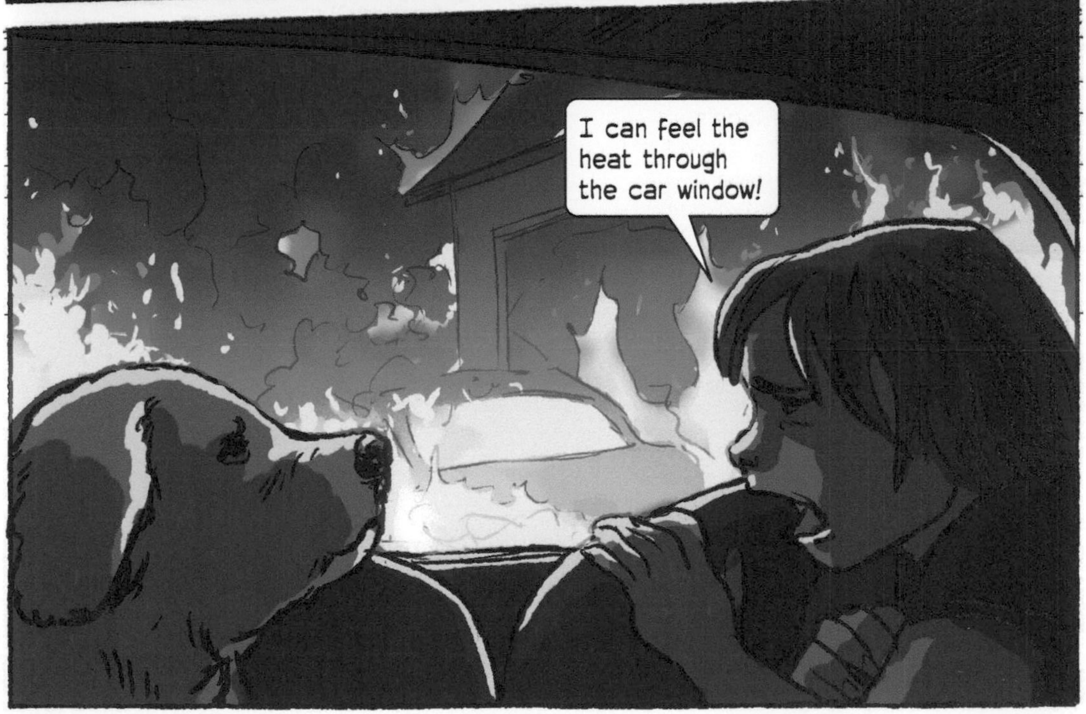
I can feel the heat through the car window!

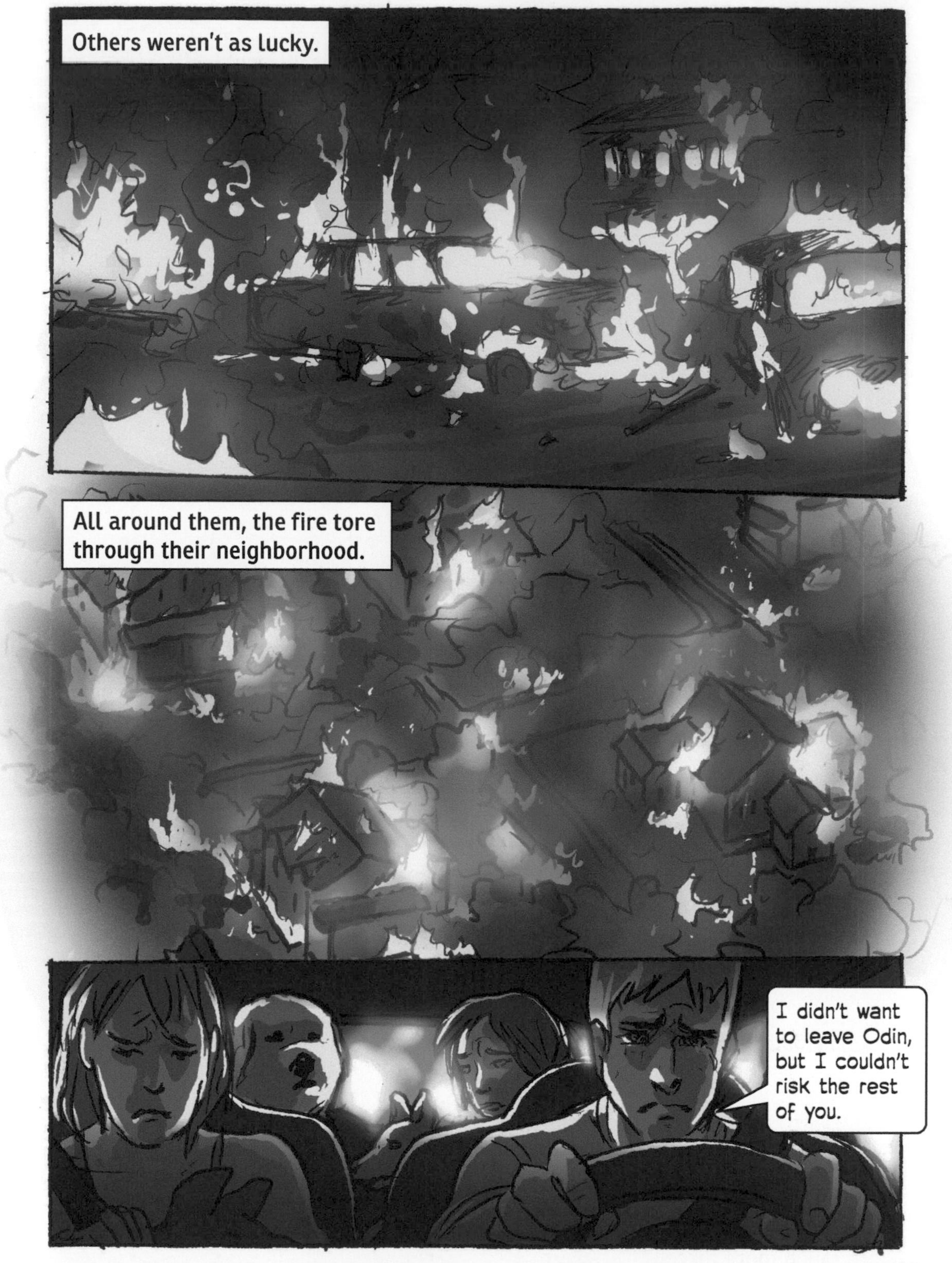
Others weren't as lucky.
All around them, the fire tore through their neighborhood.
I didn't want to leave Odin, but I couldn't risk the rest of you.

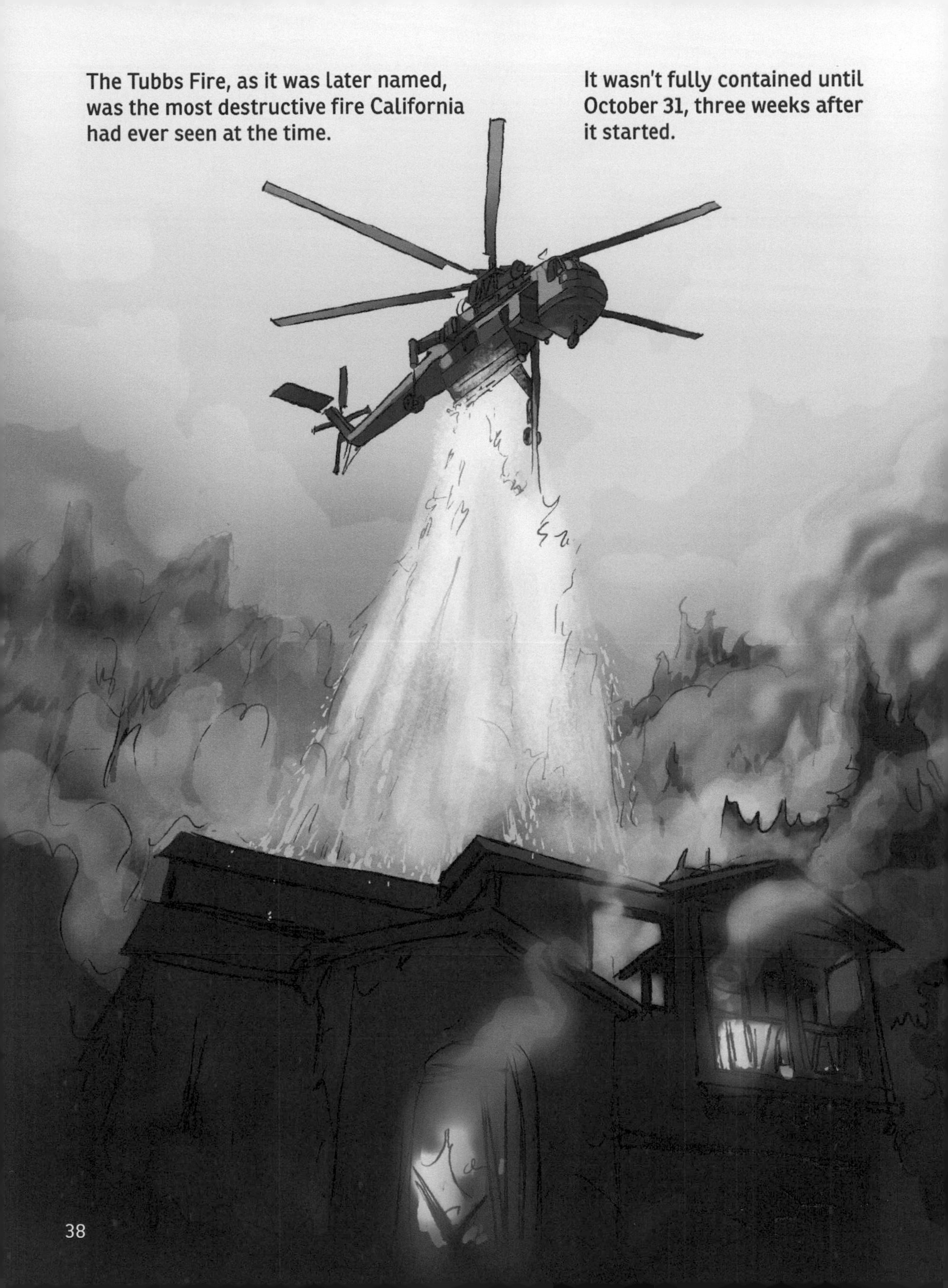
The Tubbs Fire, as it was later named, was the most destructive fire California had ever seen at the time.
It wasn't fully contained until October 31, three weeks after it started.

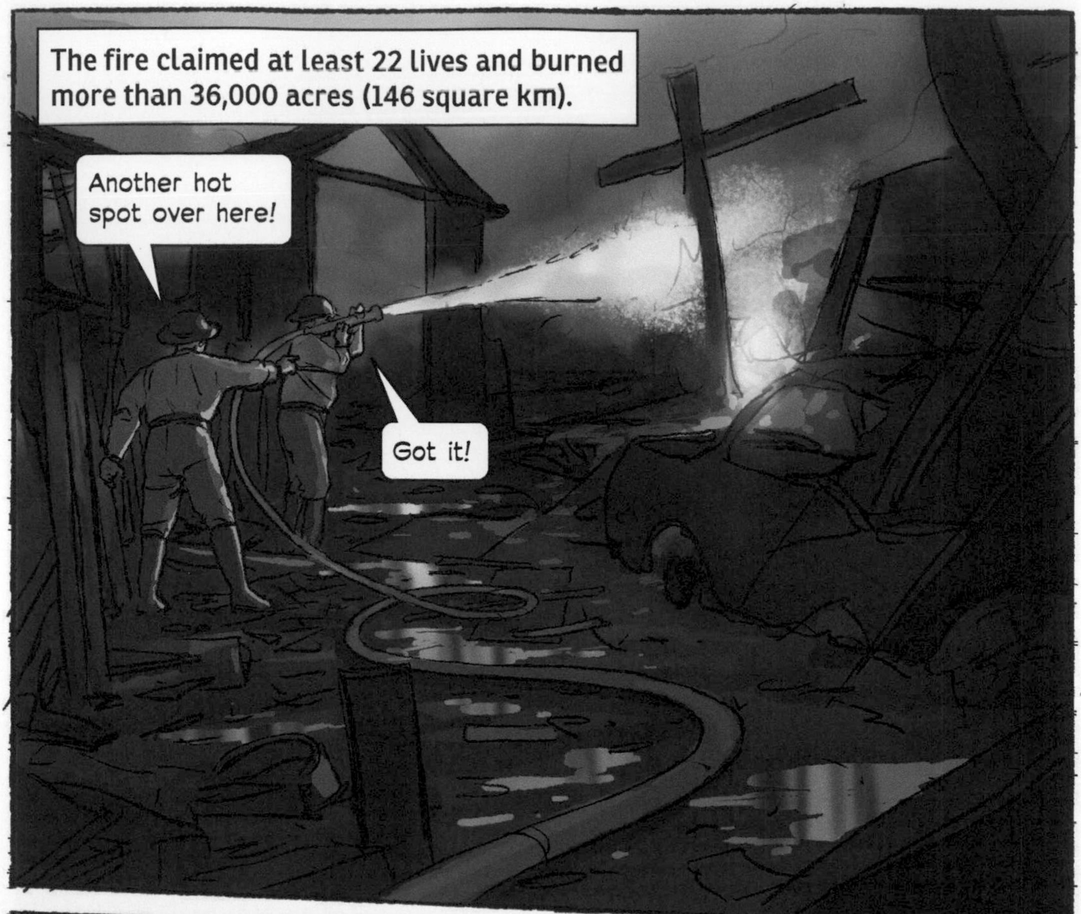
The fire claimed at least 22 lives and burned more than 36,000 acres (146 square km).
Another hot spot over here!
Got it!

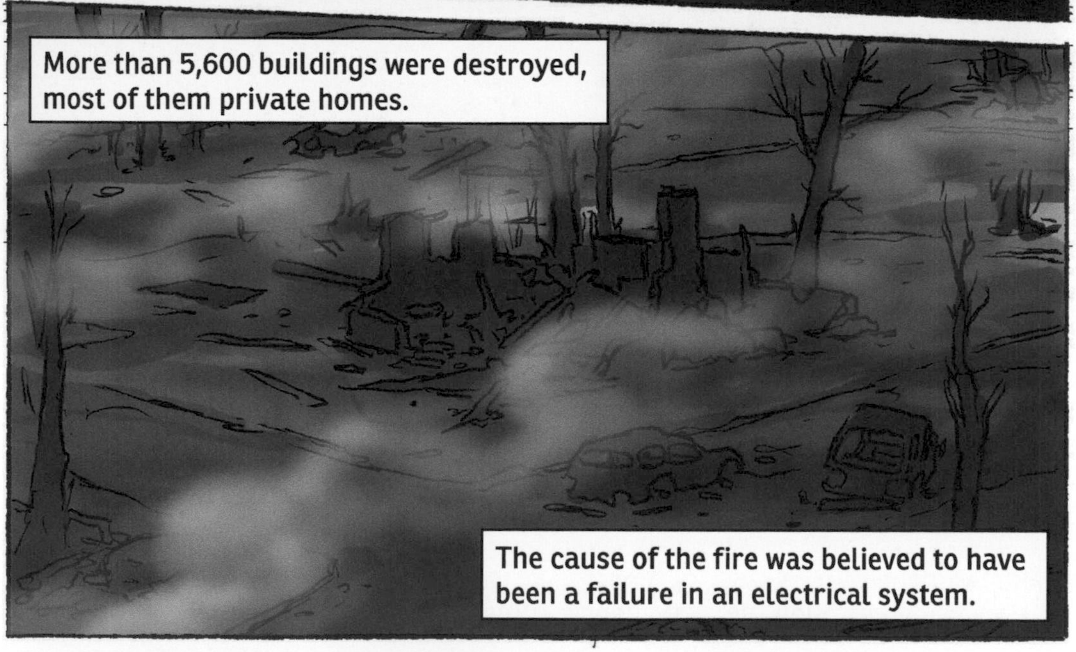
More than 5,600 buildings were destroyed, most of them private homes.
The cause of the fire was believed to have been a failure in an electrical system.

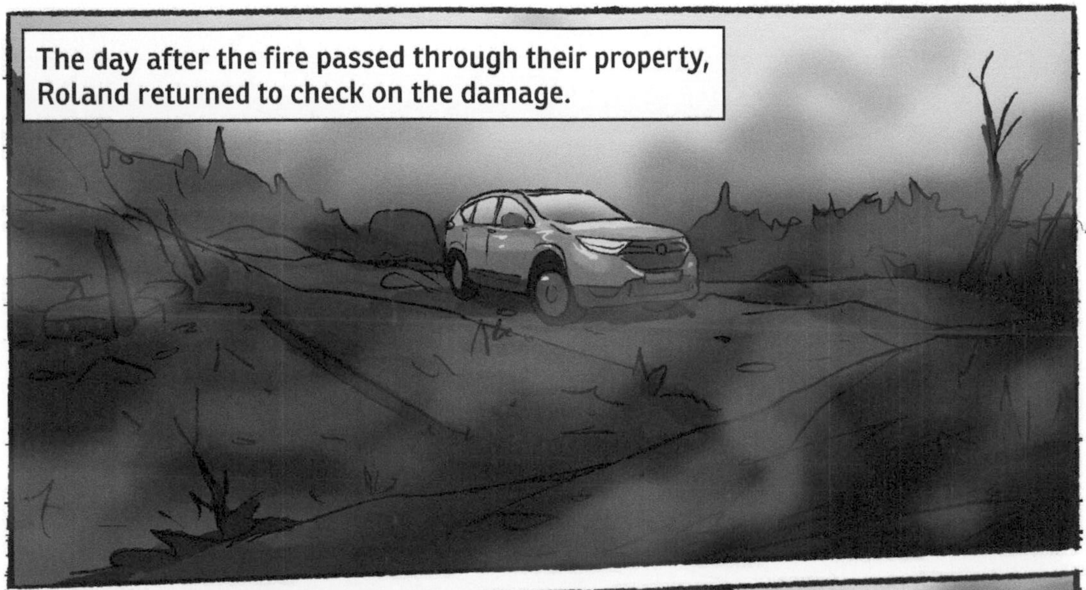
The day after the fire passed through their property, Roland returned to check on the damage.

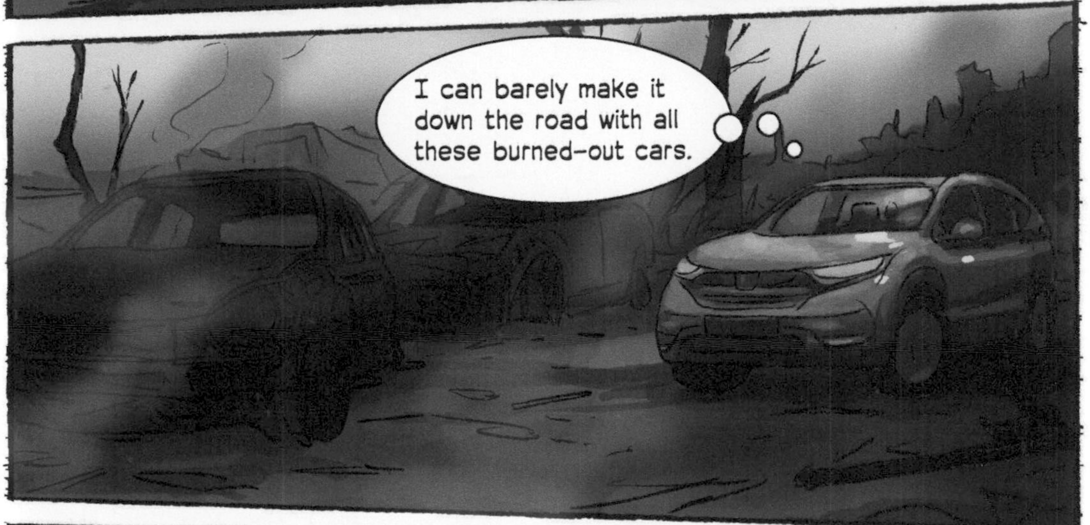
I can barely make it down the road with all these burned-out cars.

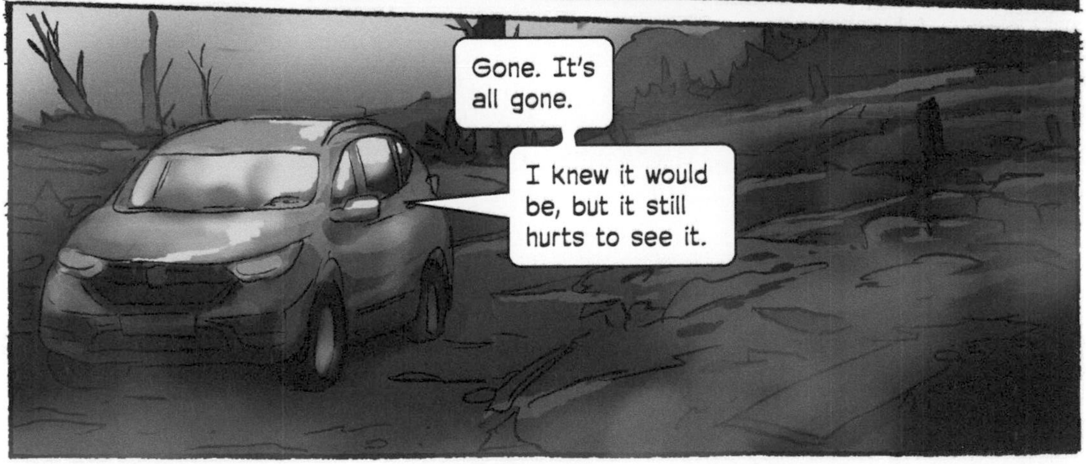
Gone. It's all gone.
I knew it would be, but it still hurts to see it.

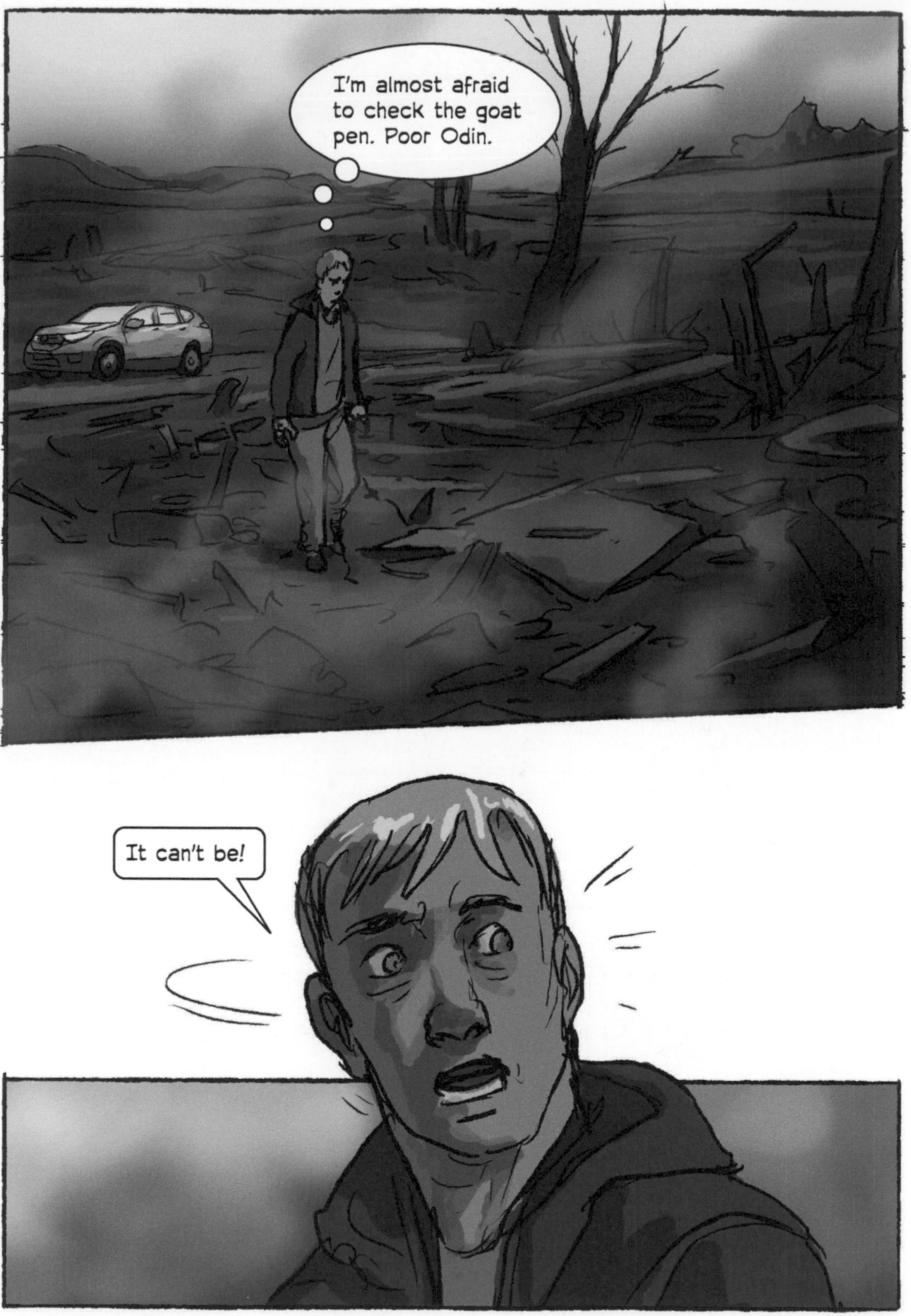
I'm almost afraid to check the goat pen. Poor Odin.
It can't be!

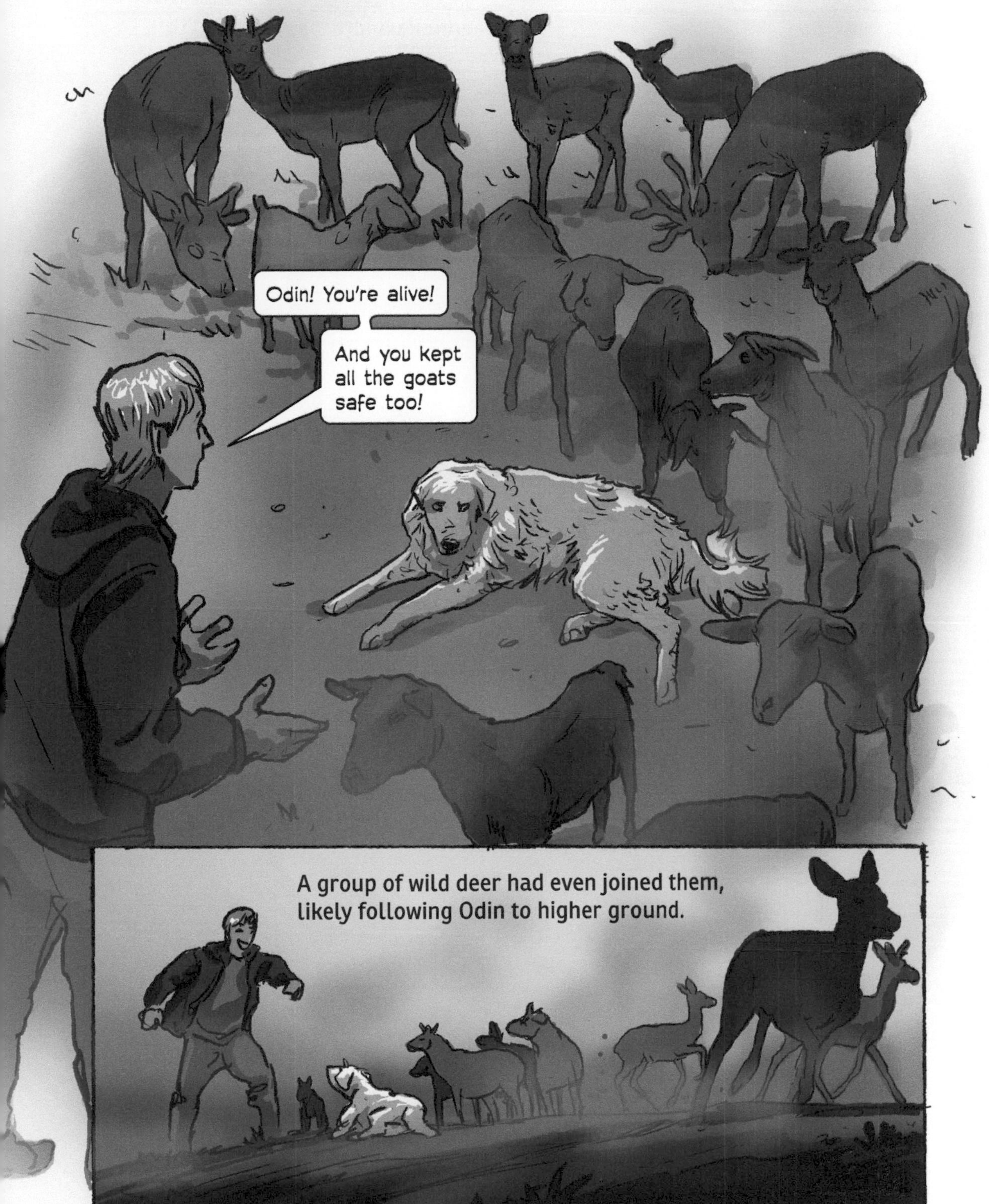
Odin! You're alive!
And you kept all the goats safe too!
A group of wild deer had even joined them, likely following Odin to higher ground.

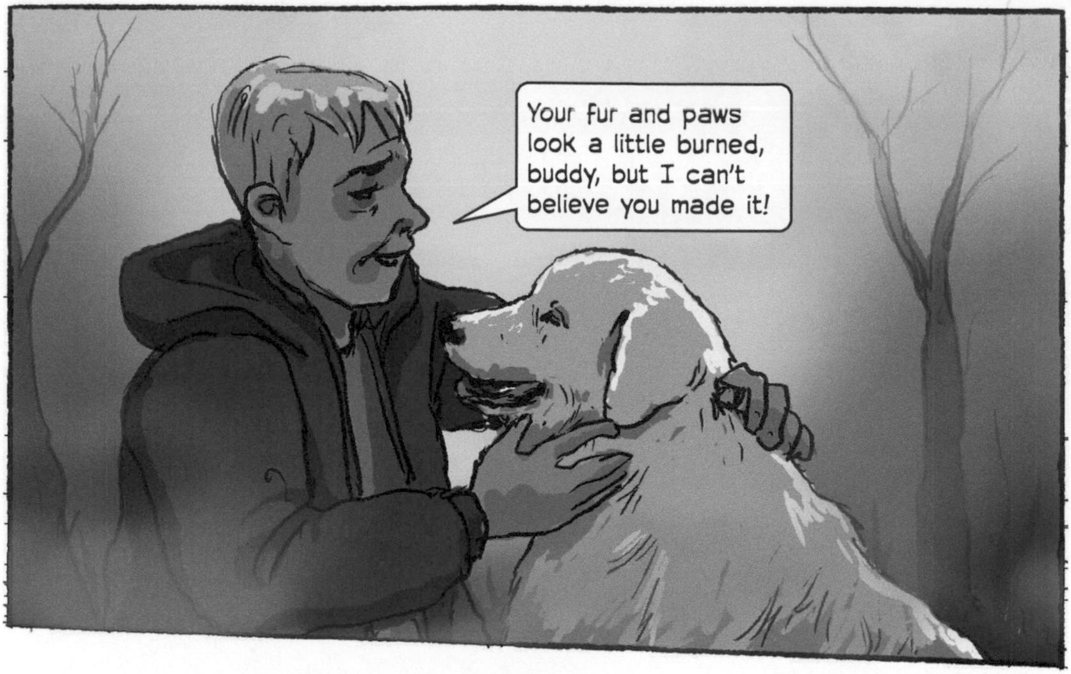
Your fur and paws look a little burned, buddy, but I can't believe you made it!

Buildings and belongings could be replaced.

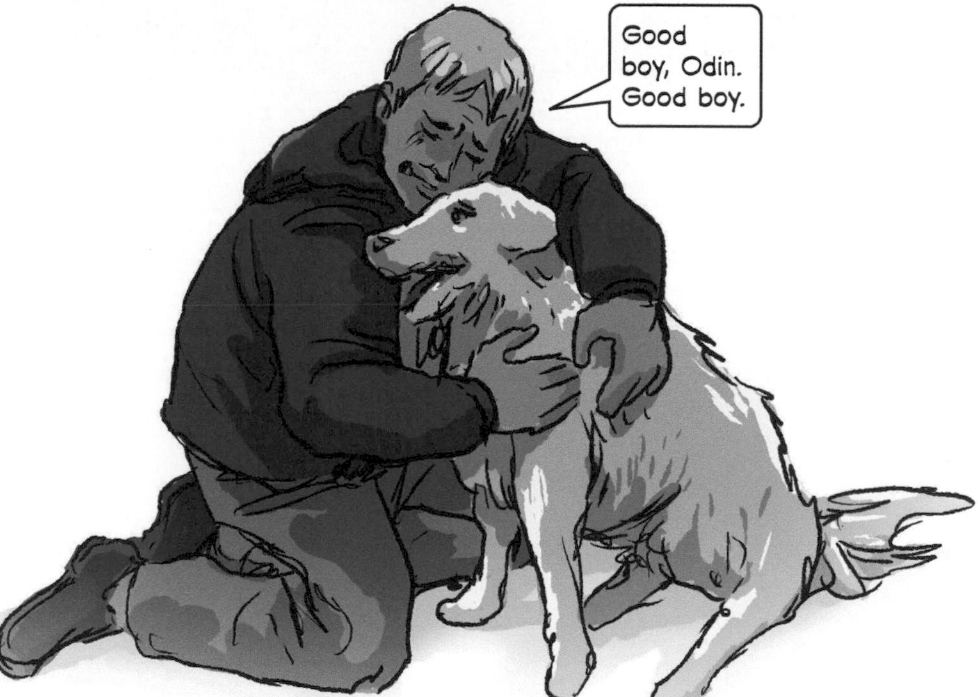
Good boy, Odin. Good boy.

The important thing was that the Hendel family had survived—all of them.

MORE ABOUT THESE TALES OF SURVIVAL

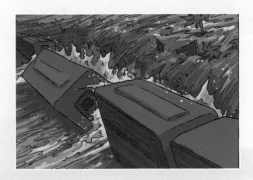

The 2004 Sumatra–Andaman earthquake is the third-largest ever recorded. The tsunami it caused reached as far as South Africa, about 5,300 miles (8,530 km) away.

On the tenth anniversary of the tsunami, Shenth Ravindra returned to Sri Lanka to remember the victims who didn't survive the disaster.

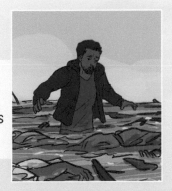

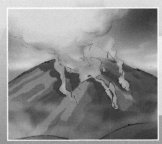

The 2014 Mount Ontake eruption was the deadliest volcanic eruption in Japan since 1926. That year, a volcanic eruption claimed 144 lives.

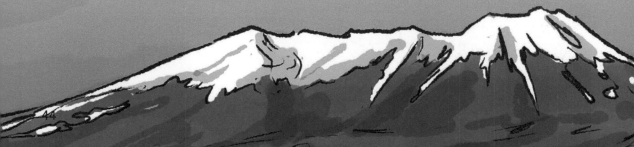